The Psychology of Work

Insights into successful working practices

Chantal Gautier

KoganPage

LONDON PHILADELPHIA NEW DELHI

First published in Great Britain and the United States in 2015 by Kogan Page Limited

2nd Floor, 45 Gee Street	1518 Walnut Street, Suite 1100	4737/23 Ansari Road
London EC1V 3RS	Philadelphia PA 19102	Daryaganj
United Kingdom	USA	New Delhi 110002
www.koganpage.com		India

© Chantal Gautier, 2015

The right of Chantal Gautier to be identified as the author of this work has been asserted by her in accordance with the Copyright, Designs and Patents Act 1988.

ISBN   978 0 7494 6834 7
E-ISBN 978 0 7494 6835 4

British Library Cataloguing-in-Publication Data

A CIP record for this book is available from the British Library.

Library of Congress Cataloging-in-Publication Data

Gautier, Chantal.
The psychology of work : insights into successful working practices / Chantal Gautier. -- 1st Edition.
    pages cm
    ISBN 978-0-7494-6834-7 (paperback) – ISBN 978-0-7494-6835-4 (e-ISBN))   1. Work–Psychological aspects.   2. Psychology, Industrial.   3. Corporate culture.   4. Employee motivation.   I. Title.
    HF5548.8.G358 2015
    158.7--dc23

                                                                                            2014047463

Typeset by Graphicraft Limited, Hong Kong
Print production managed by Jellyfish
Printed and bound by CPI Group (UK) Ltd, Croydon, CR0 4YY

CONTENTS

LIST OF FIGURES

LIST OF TABLES

ACKNOWLEDGMENTS

I would like to take this opportunity to thank my publisher for commissioning me, and the 32 industry leaders for the valuable insights they provided through their personal narratives so that we could bring the book to life.

I would also like to thank Kristy Barker, Julia Cheah, Maria Flynn, John Gazal, Deborah Husbands, Lena Kartintseva, Lejla Mandzukic-Kanic, Fiorentina Sterkaj, Haulah Zacharia and my beloved mum and dad for their ongoing support.

REVIEWERS' COMMENTARIES

This eminently readable and timely book strikes at the heart of what makes a workplace work well: its people. People matter, regardless of their place in the hierarchy or how small or complex the organization. Attitudes, emotions and behaviours create a working culture that impacts directly upon creativity and ultimately performance. Understanding how to motivate a workforce is the future of successful organizations. This book integrates key elements of organizational, business and social psychology theory that inform the creation of effective employees, teams and leaders. It provides a significant new resource for students, professionals, practitioners and general public alike. The most distinctive and successful element of this book is the way original research is used to inform theory and practice throughout.

Professor Angela Clow, University of Westminster

In the ever evolving world of work this refreshing publication narrates the journey of industrial and organizational psychology development through the years. Using an insightful blend of the theoretical and the practical, it spotlights a number of real-life work challenges as seen through the eyes of employees, teams, managers and leaders. Of interest to students and also more mature business readers seeking a useful synopsis of the classical theories related to the world of work and their application, this accessible book draws insights from a wide range of industries and occupations, and poses some interesting questions as to where we go from here in the world of work.

Mark Carter, PwC HR Services, Ireland Markets Leader

Introduction

What do organizations want from their employees and what do employees want from the organizations in which they work? How do we ensure the right fit between organizations and their employees? This book looks at the individual in the workplace, the way people work in teams, how they are led and what motivates them. Understanding these issues is vitally important for those currently leading organizations and provides an understanding of both how individuals can develop the skills that will make them valuable to the workforce and how they can be role models and drive organizational effectiveness themselves. *The Psychology of Work* draws upon a number of sources, and provides a theory-based and interesting narrative of the thoughts and feelings of people working in organizations in the United Kingdom and internationally.

A unique aspect of this book is the integration of theory with real-life narratives from experienced professionals and industry leaders that offers readers a greater understanding of actual working practices and employability issues. In addition, university students speak about their attitudes to future employment and how well prepared for the workplace they feel. The result is that the book seamlessly integrates psychological theory with personal narrative to inform all those who seek to study, create or work in a thriving organization. Since these new narratives form an inherent part of the book and are integrated throughout each chapter, a brief overview of the methodological principles in relation to sampling, data collection and analysis is provided.

The research study

Interviews

A total of 32 industry leaders took part in the study; they were employed in a variety of sectors in and outside the United Kingdom (UK). Of the 32 interviewees, 19 had national roles representing both public and private industries: the BBC, the private members' club Blacks, the British Museum (BM), Cognisess, Gaucho, Gielly Green, Hakkasan, the London School of Economics (LSE), L'Oréal, Microsoft UK, The Mill Ltd, Mitsubishi UFJ Securities, the National Theatre (NT), PGIR Limited, Rare Tea Company, The Royal Marines, Santander UK Plc, a London-based university and Wednesday. The remaining 13 interviewees represent the international companies of Accor (Belgium), Four Seasons Hotel (Egypt), University Hospital Caen (CHU) (France), IBM France, KLM (Royal Dutch Airline), Leiden University (the Netherlands), Dutch Ministry of Defense MOD (the Netherlands), NRC Handelsblad (the Netherlands), Ohad Maoz (MOD) Consulting (Israel), Studio Notarile Genghini & Associati (Italy), TrateMedia JLT (United Arab Emirates), Qantas Australia and Voith Industrial Services Inc (America).

At the outset of the interview process, 26 participants were in their current job role, while five participants had chosen to talk about their former employment role (Louise Hill, Guy Kendall, Linda DeGrow, Joris Luyendijk and Guy Samama). Following ethical approval and in order to give interviewees a more meaningful voice, we asked permission to use company names, given names and job titles. Of the 32 interviewees, only two requested pseudonyms: we have called them Samantha Faros and Maike van der Hooghen to protect their anonymity.

Surveys

The research study designed for this book also incorporates student data. This comes from a total of 103 third-year London-based university students studying BSc courses in psychology, cognitive neuroscience and law, and combined studies in psychology and criminology, psychology and sociology, psychology and youth studies or PR/advertising.

A written survey was undertaken to access the views of under-graduate students. Participants were asked to complete a questionnaire consisting of four closed and six open-ended questions. The six open-ended questions gathered more detailed data on the attitudes and opinions of the respondents on the topics of employability and attitudes towards work. The qualitative views of students were collated verbatim and are embedded primarily in Chapter 2 in parallel with industry leaders' views on employability.

Qualitative data analysis

Of the 32 industry leaders, 21 interviews were conducted face to face, recorded and transcribed verbatim. The remaining 11 interviewees were asked to document their answers in writing, due to time constraints and geographical constraints. Transcripts of the face-to-face interviews were sent to each participant for verification and approval. This process resolved any problems that may have arisen as a result of inaudible recording and/or typos by the author and accompanied transcribers.

A cross-sectional thematic analysis, as prescribed by Ely *et al* (1991), was carried out to identify recurring themes within the interview scripts. Thematic analysis is a useful investigative tool that has been widely used in qualitative research as a way to 'report experiences, meanings and the reality of participants' (Braun and Clarke, 2006: 81). The process consists of a number of stages, including familiarization with the data, coding the data and identifying and reviewing themes. Following this principle, each interviewee transcript was thoroughly read and coded line by line, and themes were identified. Themes were derived based on the prevalence of recurring patterns across the interview data set. The qualitative data sets are embedded in Chapters 2, 6 and 7.

What is the book about?

Chapter 1 provides an overview of some of the important develop-ments that underlie current theoretical perspectives on the workplace.

It provides a brief historical overview of the origins of work and how this led to the development of an approach to organizational management known as 'scientific management'. The chapter describes how later, and in reaction to this controlled yet revolutionary set of working practices, the movements of human relations and Human Resource Management emerged. This overview helps set the scene for the principles of job analysis and how this led to the development of job descriptions, both of which play an important role in current organizational practice. With a focus on recruitment and selection practices, the chapter delves into how job descriptions supposedly attract the right people to the job, and how job analysis helps the employer select the right person to fill the role.

A unique feature of Chapter 2 is its illumination of theory with tangible insights from the real world. Narratives from experienced professionals and industry leaders offer readers greater understanding of real-life working practices and employability issues. It is particularly relevant for graduates as it assists those about to embark on the journey of seeking employment in understanding how they can become more employable. This means identifying some of the key attributes (eg communication, teamwork, resilience, trustworthiness, initiative) and skill sets (eg writing skills, listening, being decisive) that employers across differing sectors look for in potential candidates. In addition, for those who develop degree courses, consideration is given to whether courses are delivering to students the skills that employers are looking for. Alongside the viewpoints of industry leaders, student narratives and data sets from the written surveys further capture the feelings and attitudes of students on the subject of work. The chapter continues with the most prominent methods of selection, with a focus on the employment interview, in particular the ways both interviewer and interviewee make sense of the process and how this can lead to unforeseen biases and decision-making errors. Suggestions are made about how this can be managed. The chapter closes by explaining the links to recruitment practices and workplace romances, with the suggestion that organizations may unwittingly and indirectly be responsible for creating the perfect playground for romantic fraternization.

One of the keystones of organizational life is working with other people, with the idea that 'together everyone achieves more'. Chapter 3 thus introduces the concept of teams and how they develop, suggesting that the majority of teams pass through five stages before they reach their ultimate peak in performance. The chapter also explores the role of team leader, considering the wider context in which teams are created alongside the relevant team-related ingredients that will promote effective teamworking practices. The chapter recognizes that some people are perceived as non-team players, and some reasons for this are discussed in Chapter 4.

On the back of team development theories and their psychological underpinnings, Chapter 4 provides a glimpse as to the reasons why teams fail. Explanations are sought in the sphere of social psychology, with a focus on groupthink and conformity. A further example is drawn from the concept of 'social loafing', and more importantly why certain team members do not contribute. The chapter argues that despite the many barriers, with the right team intervention tools even the most dysfunctional teams can work. It surmises that, despite the inconclusive research on the benefits and pitfalls of teams, on the whole teamwork is fundamental to organizational life.

For teams to work successfully, organizations must foster a culture that supports them. With this in mind, the main focus of Chapter 5 is on the different variants of culture and how these manifest themselves. It is suggested that each culture holds a unique sets of rituals, habits and symbols that direct the ways people will behave to one another. Organizations will be looking to recruit people who will fit their particular culture: that is, share similar values and other distinct patterns of the organization. In closing, the chapter proposes that sustainable cultures are characterised by practising what they preach, empowering members by giving them decision-making latitude, varied work and control over what they do.

At the forefront of organizational psychology is the study of leadership. Chapter 6 examines a number of key questions: What is leadership? What makes leaders effective and what specific abilities and traits do they possess? In addressing these questions, the chapter provides an overview of the classic leadership theories and discusses whether leadership is an innate quality or one that can be learnt.

The book's final chapter presents new research findings on how to improve working practices and relationships. In doing so it offers a wide range of practical and theoretical guidance on how that can be achieved. It is particularly significant for those completing studies who are, or hope to be, the leaders of the future. First, there is a discussion of what motivates people and how this affects the construct of the psychological contract. While most workplace contracts are legally binding, we explain that non-written agreements (eg career progression, training or promotion opportunities) are also negotiated between employers and employees. Attention will also be paid to what happens when employees believe that unwritten mutual exchanges and expectations have not been respected, which may lead to a string of emotional triggers, including demotivation. In closing, new insights and suggestions about how to improve today's workplace are provided through the newly proposed humanistic-based model of emotional intelligence leadership. This model challenges the status quo, arguing that people are more than just cogs in a machine. This insight demands our attention as well as reminding us of the significance of bringing the 'humane' back into organizational life.

This book is the result of a career working in organizational psychology, higher education and research with a range of professionals and industry leaders. It is written with a wide audience in mind, including students, professionals and anyone with an interest in how successful organizations operate. In studying the subject matter it provides the key theoretical frameworks of organizational psychology as well as practical tips for individual employees, teams, managers and leaders. It is particularly relevant to students at both undergraduate and postgraduate level following degree courses in psychology, organizational psychology, MBAs, business and management, as well as researchers in these areas.

Recruitment and selection

01

The focus of this chapter will be on the recruitment and selection side of Human Resource Management (HRM). Recruitment and selection practices are crucial in building an organization's internal labour pool and are linked to success and competitive advantage. The chapter will describe how jobs are created through the practice of job analysis, and discuss the data collection methodologies that lead to job descriptions. It will argue that if potential recruits grasp the psychology behind recruitment, this helps them to identify the work and worker-related requirements for any given job. The chapter begins with a brief historical account of the lead-up to the birth of HRM.

Historical background

Until the 18th century, most work was carried out by farming families who lived off agriculture and the land. Later, new socioeconomic and technological interventions and innovations in engineering put Britain at the vanguard of the Industrial Revolution. This was made possible by increased natural/energy resources and technological changes, which ultimately led to the mass production of manufactured goods. Meanwhile, Adam Smith (1723–90), keen to explore the potential of capitalism, concluded that wealth could only increase through the division of labour, with a focus on reducing costs by enhancing and standardizing production. Before long, the new ideas about division of labour and specialization of function (ie converting skilled crafts into a series of simplified divisible jobs) gave rise to the 'factory system' (Smith, 2007).

For traditional craftspeople, these new ideas triggered a major change in how work was to be organized. While such workers had had almost complete autonomy over how and when to work, now people were not only forced to learn a new set of work skills to operate machinery, but also suddenly confined to working within the demands of more routinized and capital-intensive 'factory systems'. Before long, a new science in how to manage workers and labour gave birth to what became known as the study of scientific management.

In the early stages of studying the behaviour of people in organizations across Europe and the United States, a handful of researchers showed an interest in the field of psychological sciences. The discipline of the psychological sciences came of age in 1892 with the founding of the American Psychological Association (APA), instigated by Stanley Hall and his colleagues. They were following in the footsteps of Wilhelm Wundt (1839–1920), known as the 'Father of Psychology' and renowned for having built the first experimental psychology laboratory at Columbia University. James Cattell (1860–1944) was the first professor of psychology in the United States to study the concept of individual differences within psychophysical settings. Cattell devised what became known as the 'mental test' (1890). Meanwhile, French psychologist Binet (1905), co-founder of the Binet and Simon (1908) intelligence scale, was also preoccupied with the field of mental testing.

Outside the traditional sphere, Walter Dill Scott (1869–1955) became known as the first researcher to apply experimental psychology in the workplace, while Munsterberg (1913) sought to understand the mechanisms of 'worker fatigue' and 'work potential' and their direct links with job satisfaction; similarly, Myers (1929) and Hausmann (1931) examined the relationship between job satisfaction and motivation. Despite the research efforts across continents, however, it was not until after the First World War that the field of industrial psychology really took off. The first industrial psychological prompt came when Stanley Hall suggested psychologists could assist the US military in their selection practices. Joint efforts led to the development of the Army Alpha test (alongside Beta test programmes for those who could not read). Their success in the selection of army officers established the roles of organizational psychologists. Later, with the new arrival of governing bodies in the form of the Psychology Committee of the National Resource Council and the Committee on Classification and Personnel, selection practices began to take form. From this point onwards, industrial psychologists were, step by step, able to demonstrate the benefits of applied psychology, and how it could enhance organizational effectiveness.

Scientific management

In close parallel with Adam Smith's ideas, in 1911 industrial engineer Frederick Taylor made his visionary offering to the field with a focus on how to improve worker productivity. Taylor's ideas focused on the optimization of tasks and simplification of work. This simplification, Taylor explained, allowed workers to perform in the most efficient manner. To determine the optimal method, Taylor performed time studies, using a stopwatch to time a worker's sequence of motions. Through systematically observing individual operations, Taylor was able to break down each job component into specialized sequences of motions, ranging from small to larger tasks. By evaluating the 'sum of their parts', Taylor identified the most efficient methods: that is, those involving least expenditure of human energy. Taylor believed it was up to managers to monitor and drive workers to higher productivity levels, and so began the introduction of managerial controls. The new methods implied that workers were left with no autonomy and no opportunity to make decisions, were treated simply as 'cogs in a machine'. Needless to say, this soon bred discontent among the workforce. Workers opposed not only their conditions of work but also the continuous repetition of isolated, monotonous activities. With the rise of trade unions the fight for better working conditions took a new form, which ultimately led to the major study at the Hawthorne plant of the Western Electric Company in Chicago.

Hawthorne studies

While scientific management did lay the foundation for the study of work behaviour, it was criticized for its disregard of welfare and the worker: Taylor simply saw workers as a means to an end. Humanization of work did not evolve until the revelation of data from the Hawthorne studies carried out at Western Electric's factory. Australian-born Elton Mayo (1880–1949) began to explore the factors that affect worker productivity, and the Hawthorne study (1927–33) factored in a number of environmental changes. These included improvements in lighting, as well as longer breaks and adjustments to working hours.

The study succeeded in establishing the best working methods but also presented an unexpected finding regarding social context. It showed that when workers are given freedom to make decisions and the opportunity to discuss their working practices, it is this that truly incentivizes them, rather than a change in lighting or other ergonomic aspects. It appears that Mayo was not alone in his thinking, since similarities have also been detected in Karasek's (1979) Job Demands Control Model, which we will return to and discuss in Chapter 5.

The Hawthorne studies coined the term 'Hawthorne Effect': the notion that higher productivity is the result of an improvement in human relations between workers and managers rather than changes of an environmental nature (Jones, 1990). Mayo (1945: 111) argues that 'man's desire to be continuously associated in work with his fellows is a strong, if not the strongest, human characteristic.' Thus it was concluded that it is not sufficient to simply study tasks and duties; rather, it is necessary to include the interpersonal, group co-herence and humane elements, and to bring back the humane into organizational life.

Human resource management

The human relations movement was the first to focus on the behaviours of people working in groups and the impact this had on individual performance, motivation and job satisfaction. In the 1960s and 1970s the movement gained impetus from Carl Rogers (1951) and Abraham Maslow (1954), who together pioneered the Humanistic Movement and provided the setting for Humanistic Psychology. Rogers (1961) contributed further towards the human relations movement by bringing the need for human interactions to the forefront of the study of organizational theory. This effectively shaped the beginnings of Human Resource Management (HRM) as a reaction to the scientific approaches to work. The HRM framework was underpinned by recognizing the efforts of an organization's people and the value of human capital. This meant understanding the necessary skill sets of people in order to keep organizations thriving. Further along it was believed that recognizing the value of human resources could lead to greater competitive advantage, defined here as 'the ability to generate above normal returns relative to competitors' (Ployhart, 2012: 62). With this in mind, SHRM (Strategic Human Resource Management) developed a strategic approach towards work, with a focus on how to acquire, manage, develop and motivate people so as to promote high performance workplaces (Miller, 1987). This meant devising strategies to manage human capital where important decisions are made about people. The chapter will move on to discuss the recruitment and selection side of SHRM, and the people who are tasked with aligning the right candidates to the organization and its goals (Catano, 2012). The first discussion point involves the process of job analysis, followed by the job description and person specification.

Job analysis

For an organization to run effectively, thought must be given to its recruitment and selection processes. Recruitment is concerned with attracting the right people to apply for a vacancy, while selection involves choosing job candidates from a previously generated pool (Catano, 2012). In addressing the selection process, work psychology relies on a process called job analysis, which is the systematic approach through which information about a job is gathered (Sackett and Laczo, 2003). This process results in two sets of data: job description and job specification. In achieving this, two distinct yet separate areas need to examined: worker-orientated and work-orientated information. The first focuses on the person and the behavioural and psychological elements required for people to be good at their job (Sandberg, 2000). The second involves information about the work involved, with a focus on procedures, resources and equipment usage, as well as the physical layout of the job, its environment and where it is positioned in the organizational hierarchy.

In gathering work and worker-orientated information, quantitative and qualitative data collection techniques help yield detailed information about knowledge, skills, abilities and other characteristics (KSAOs) relevant to the job. As it is beyond the scope of this chapter to consider all methods, a handful of techniques will be highlighted.

Data collection

Quantitative techniques

The questionnaire is one method used by job analysts in gathering and dissecting job-related information. The Position Analysis Questionnaire (PAQ) developed by McCormick and Jeanneret (1988) is the most widely used worker-orientated standardized measure, comprising a list of 300 elements. Elements are organized into six categories across 2,200 jobs, including 'information input, mental processes, work output, relationship with others, job context, other job characteristics' (Deb, 2009: 136). The elements collate information about the responsibilities and duties of the job and about worker-orientated attributes. While the PAQ is not intended to measure proficiency, criticisms have been raised concerning its generic elements, suggesting that those these may well be applicable to jobs that are similar to one another, they do not apply across different kinds of jobs (see, for example, Jones *et al*, 1982).

The Functional Job Analysis (FJA) questionnaire devised by Fine (1955) was initially used by the US Department of Labor and served as a job classification basis for the Dictionary of Occupational Titles (DOT), though it has now been replaced with the online O*NET system. Like the PAQ, it focuses on worker-orientated information that is specific to what workers do in jobs. The FJA uses seven scales to describe reasoning, language, verbal ability, mathematical, analytical and judgement skills.

The Work Profiling System (WPS) devised by Saville and Holdsworth (1995) is a structured computer-administrated questionnaire that measures ability and personality attributes such as hearing skills, sight, taste, smell, touch, body coordination, number skills, complex management skills, verbal skills, personality and teamwork. This questionnaire is helpful for employees who work in technical and/or in managerial roles.

The Job Component Inventory (JCI) developed by Banks and Miller (1984) was primarily created to assist in the development of vocational programmes and career guidance. The inventory lists 220 items related to six dimensions: use of tools and equipment, and physical/perceptual, mathematical, communication, decision-making and responsibility requirements.

Qualitative techniques

Alongside the use of questionnaires, it is also necessary to draw upon a range of qualitative data collection techniques. Written materials (eg job descriptions) can be used as a valuable starting point for the job analyst to build on. However, unless job descriptions are regularly updated, existing descriptions may miss out important job-related information, particularly when jobs' roles change over time.

The use of diaries is another qualitative technique used in yielding job-related information. Here the jobholders are asked to keep a record of their working practices over a typical working day. However, unless jobholders can identify and reflect upon important aspects of their work, information may turn out to be subjective. Identifying these elements requires time and thought, leading to the risk that the individual may not begin this process until shortly before the deadline and may then complete it from memory. Nonetheless, Carter and Mankoff (2005) claim that the diary entry method can be effective and time-efficient when recordings are carried out through the use of 'digital capture media'.

The Critical Incident Technique devised by Flanagan (1954) invites workers to identify critical incidents associated with either good or poor performance. Incidents are examined in terms of how well or poorly the jobholder handled a specific situation. Though the method is useful in a job analysis exercise, problems can arise in the way information is disclosed. Jobholders may tend to attribute poor performance to external cues rather than to themselves. This so-called 'cardinal attribution error', explains Doyle (2003), can cause potential biases or lose sight of important information that may prove central to the job.

The observation or shadowing method has the benefit that jobholders are observed in their natural working environments (see for example Arnold, 2005). In this context, observers can study physical layout and equipment usage. In some instances however, jobholders are said to deliberately adjust their behaviours, meaning important job components may be left out or unknown to the observer. Another problem with this method concerns the analyst's skill in recording job-related observations, and having the resources or time to do so.

To sum up, job analysis is key to the selection process as it helps identify the appropriate KSAOs. To ensure a 'customized synthesis' of data, job analysts, occupational psychologists and HR professionals understand it is necessary to adopt a multi-faceted methodological approach. The next step is to create job descriptions and person specifications.

Job description

Job descriptions provide important information about organizational structure and responsibilities, as well as functional information (ie what the work is). While there is no prescribed template as such, the following job specific headings should be in some shape or form visible:

- job title;
- purpose;
- principal duties;
- direct line of report;

- working conditions;
- holiday entitlement;
- salary range.

When studying job descriptions, it is surprising how many are found to be incomplete. This lack of detailed information can cause problems for both recruiters and their potential candidates. For example, at an individual level, adverts that leave out important information make it difficult for the job seekers to make sense of what is asked of them. As a result employers risk attracting the wrong applicants. At the organizational level, incomplete job adverts may unwittingly send a negative message to the outside world, the message being that the organization is disorganized and lacks efficiency and attention to detail. With the advances in technology and wealth of information available to recruitment officers, there is no good reason why job adverts should be poorly presented.

Person specifications follow from the job description and identify the qualifications, personal skills, knowledge, abilities, experience and other requirements to successfully perform the job. Rodger's (1952) seven-point listing is still the one most commonly used in creating person specifications.

- attainment;
- general intelligence;
- special aptitudes;
- disposition;
- circumstances;
- physical characteristics;
- interests.

Attainment reflects what educational background, training and experience is required for the job. It also includes membership of professional bodies. *General intelligence* applies to the applicant's intellectual capability. *Special aptitudes* are the tailored demands specific to the job, such as analytical, artistic, reasoning or numerical abilities. *Disposition* is generally concerned with personality and includes such things as relationships with people, reliability, conscientiousness and self-assurance. *Circumstances* relates to whether the person is able to meet necessary conditions for the job, such as the need for travel or shift work. *Physical characteristics* involve health, speech, grooming and appearance. The seventh component, *interests*, involves the applicant's interest areas, including sports, culture or hobbies.

Having presented the foundations of job analysis and how this leads to job descriptions and person specifications, the next stage to consider is selection. The selection panel should comprise an eclectic group who are either directly involved in the recruitment process (eg human resource officers) or directly involved with the job role (eg managers and peers members). Most selection processes involve three main stages: first, it requires candidates to supply biographical information and a Curriculum Vitae (CV). If both fulfil the selection criteria, candidates enter the second stage: the interview. The third stage includes the request for references. The successful outcome of the stages leads to the job offer, which involves the candidate's acceptance or decline of the position. The process requires careful consideration from both parties.

Attention will now be paid to a handful of the most common selection methods used. Particular attention will be paid to the employment interview.

Selection and assessment methods

The very first example of personnel selection was seen in China, when Han Emperor Wu founded the 'imperial examination' in 605 AD to select the best administrators for the state bureaucracy (Elman, 2002). The selection process was ahead of its time: it was without constraints and open to anyone, regardless of position or status. Today's recruitment challenge involves a wider range of selection methods and is more complex in design than previously. Evidence shows that the use of tests is still widespread across sectors, as shown in an IRS survey (2009). Of the 90 organizations surveyed (employing approximately 420,000 people), 85 per cent reported the use of tests for recruitment and selection purposes. In particular, tests were geared towards measurements of personality, attitudes and behaviours (IRS, 2009), though organizational psychologists understand it is difficult to precisely predict how potential applicants are likely to perform. Henrietta Lovell, founder of the Rare Tea Company, affirms that it is sometimes difficult to recruit the right person, admitting: 'you cannot always get it right the first time round. Fundamentally, it is about selecting the right person that fits the team.' Organizations still get it wrong – even when candidates fulfil the criteria sets, this does not necessarily guarantee a match. The question is how do we know if someone is the right fit? Santander UK's Director of Human Resources Simon Lloyd explains: 'we are administering some psychological testing and competency-based interviewing. We do a number of assessment centres and role-playing.' Similarly Human Resource Director Isabelle Minneci of L'Oréal suggests using a combination of elements:

> it starts with whether the candidate has the right level of experience, skills and competencies for the job we recruit. Then we also look at cultural fit. Each company has a different culture and it is important that a candidate can adapt and embrace the company culture; this is often a question of personality, shared values, ways of working.

In this quest, two models are used: first, the Person Job-fit (Edwards, 1991), which is focused on fitting the person (ie matching the applicant's KSAs) to the required job demands. The Person Organization-fit (Kristof, 1996) Model, meanwhile, seeks to identify a person's values, beliefs or interests and whether these form a match to the culture of the given organization (Bowen, Ledford and Nathan, 1991). In finding the right cultural match, Chief Creative Officer, and Co-Founder of the Mill, Pat Joseph explains that sometimes there is a mismatch between candidates and the given organization's ethos:

> though we did have the most A-graded character come in... we had to cease his tenure after one month, not because he was not brilliant... but he did not learn anything... he missed understanding the fact that there are other talented people here and respecting that. The best thing to know is that you are great, but not the greatest in the world; if you cannot accept that then you cannot succeed in any business because it is collaborative.

While the ultimate aim is to align the right candidate early in the selection process, sometimes it is not until the candidate starts work that either party (the candidate or the organization) realizes that it is not a suitable match after all.

The central question remains: what are the psychological principles that underpin successful selection practices? Chris Butt, CEO of Cognisess, believes it is about 'good recruitment policy, and you need to look after people; you need to make things clear and simple. It is about building your talent pool correctly.' Chris adds:

> All too often companies will do some profile and assessment, but do nothing with that information. It is a continuous process.

After all, Chris notes: 'a company's most valuable asset is its people – 75 per cent of the intellectual property (IP) and value is tied up in the heads of its employees. If this is understood and driven at board or senior level then the human resources team can facilitate change more rapidly.' This means, understanding what types of people are needed in the organization.

The discussion will now move on to highlight the different selection and assessment methods, beginning with biographical information, followed by assessment centres, psychometric tests, interviews and references.

Biographical information

Biographical data is often used as a first point of call (or sometimes post-interview for the purpose of background checks) and concerns personal historical data. This usually includes a person's age, gender, date of birth, marital status, religion and ethnicity, and past experience, education, training and so on. Under the Equality Act (2010), it is unlawful to discriminate on grounds of age, sex, disability or race. This means employers will be expected to act with caution and integrity in the sampling and/or storing of biographical data. In recruitment and selection practices, candidates must therefore be made aware why they are asked provide such information.

The bio-data approach can be useful in trying to predict job success, as each item is given an importance in weighting. The aim is to match the most appropriate biographical information with the outcome measures of the job. While this does have its merits, it is suggested that the approach is rather laborious as well as time-intensive (Torrington *et al*, 2014). This perhaps is why the method is chiefly used in large organizations where high volumes of vacancies are advertised. Although the method has its uses, biographical data has been criticised for its low predictive validity score of 0.35 (Cook, 2009).

Assessment centres

In some cases, organizations will outsource their selection practices to what is referred to as an assessment centre. This is sometimes done explains Ployhart (2012) for cost-cutting purposes, but the main rationale behind assessment centres is that they provide applicants not with one single selection method, but rather a variety of selection batches. For this reason, the method is said to best capture the unique abilities of candidates (Cook, 2009) and measure a particular characteristic or trait on parameters surrounding validity and reliability. A wide range of methods is thus incorporated in helping to identify the desired competencies of each candidate. Typically these include the ability to relate to others, leadership, motivation, written and verbal communication, problem-solving, organizing, planning and emotional stability.

One assessment centre practice includes work sample tests or simulated tests. These are used in simulating on-the-job situations. For example, a bartender may be asked to demonstrate his or her knowledge or creativeness by mixing a particular cocktail. An academic may be asked to give a presentation to help assess his or her presentation abilities. Or a personal assistant may be asked to type a letter in a required time frame. Time limits may be enforced in order to simulate the time pressure experienced in real life and to assess accuracy. Scoring sheets are then reviewed via computerized templates or by trainers who have closely monitored the candidate's performance. Other exercises are geared towards helping to assess the candidates' ability to manage, multi-skill, prioritize, delegate and/or analyse information quickly (Smith and Smith, 2005).

Role-play exercises are also used in work-sampling scenarios, often so as to capture a candidate's interpersonal style. Role-play exercises are used to simulate particular scenarios and to identify potential competencies. For example, candidates may be assessed on their communication and interpersonal styles. Prior to the role-play exercise, candidates are given a script with background information about the scenario and role they are expected to act out. Actors – ie trained role-players – often participate in such scenarios. During the role-play, exercise performance is observed and later evaluated on the basis of criteria directly related to the requirements of the job.

Assessment centres are generally considered to offer a fair process because all candidates carry out the same tests. Similarly, because assessment centre exercises involve a mixture of both individual and group-related activities, it is suggested that they provide equal opportunities for all candidates: each candidate is assessed independently. Assessors are drawn from both outside (eg psychologists are usually bought in to administer tests, observe candidates and/or make recommendations) and inside (ranging from practising senior managers to non-managerial jobholders), and adopt what is known as the ORCE (Observe, Record, Classify and Evaluate) approach. The ORCE approach provides assessors with a structured framework, enabling them to act as consistently as possible throughout the evaluation process (Edenborough, 2005).

Psychometric tests

Psychometrics are widely used in selection procedures, as they are good performance indicators, mainly because they are standardized. A psychometric test that shows *criterion*-related validity is one that has demonstrated its effectiveness in predicting the criterion of a construct. In other words, a test is said to have criterion-related validity when it reflects a certain set of abilities. Tests that do so, explains Edenborough (2005), show validity. When a test's results are confirmed by comparison with known criteria, we speak of *concurrent* validity. Meanwhile, tests that are perceived (by the tester) as credible are seen to have *face* validity (Robertson and Smith, 2001), and lastly when alignment exists between test questions and content area, we speak of *content* validity.

Generally, psychometric tests fall into two categories: aptitude/cognitive and personality tests. Aptitude tests measure overall reasoning or specific elements of ability such as verbal, numeric, spatial and abstract reasoning. Verbal ability tests how well candidates can communicate. Numerical ability tests general arithmetic, be it number sequences, percentages, understanding tables, charts and graphs. Spatial ability determines a candidate's potential to perceive a static figure in different positions. Abstract reasoning aims to measure one's ability to learn new things. In doing so, answers will point towards the candidate's potential to identify the underlying logic of patterns and their ability to solve problems. Flexibility measures how well someone can perform under strict deadlines or under pressure. Examples of aptitude tests include the Wechsler Adult Intelligent Scale (WAIS), which measures intelligence, and the General Aptitude Test Battery (GATB), measuring nine aptitudes.

The trait approach to personality is one of the major theoretical areas in the study of personality, described by Child (1968: 83) as 'more or less stable, internal factors that make one person's behaviour consistent from one time to another, and different from the behaviour other people would manifest in comparable situations'. Personality not only determines how we do things but also why we do it. Industry leader Simon Lloyd of Santander, after explaining that 'for customer-facing roles, we are looking for people who can relate to customers,' brings up this difficulty, adding: 'you can teach people how to use computers etc, but you cannot teach them how to be empathetic.' Since some argue (eg Eysenck, 1995) that traits are stable, this raises the question of whether, as the saying goes, you can't teach an old dog new tricks. It would appear that trait theorists think not. This raises questions about attitudes, defined here by Rosenberg *et al* (1960) as 'predispositions to respond to some class of stimuli with certain classes of response'. Psychological theories of attitudes suggest that the forming and changing of attitudes involves complex processes and depend on many different factors (Hogg and Vaughan, 2010). It is said that individual differences and situational contingencies will also determine a person's willingness to change. In the context of work this means that employers, like Human Resource Director Isabelle Minneci, will be keener to recruit candidates who are 'open, flexible as well as humble', and hence able to adjust their viewpoints and attitudes, rather than those who come across as arrogant or too full of themselves.

Needless to say, understanding how personality influences behaviour and performance is said to help attract the right person for the job. Personality tests are used to measure where the candidate sits on personality dimensions and are mostly administered through questionnaires and/or inventories. For example, the Big-Five Model explores individual characteristics to determine a personality type from the scales of extraversion, conscientiousness, agreeableness, neuroticism and openness (Costa and McCrae, 1992). The inventory is said to help predict work-related behaviours such as performance, leadership and motivation. For example, conscientiousness measures individuals' attributes of persistence, motivation and responsibility, all of which directly impact working practices (Barrick and Mount, 1991). Similarly, Cattell's (1946) Sixteen Personality Factor (16PF) and Eysenck's Personality Questionnaire (EPQ) are used in teasing out the relevant trait sets jobholders may have. The requirements will of course vary from job to job. The 16PF measures 16 traits (eg social attitudes, intelligence) while the EPQ measures three (neuroticism–stability, introversion–extraversion and psychoticism–normality). It is suggested that while both questionnaires demonstrate good test–retest reliability, the 16PF is less valid than the EPQ (Arnold, 2005). Other personality tests include the Occupational Personality Questionnaire (OPQ32) devised by Saville and Holdsworth, and the Hogan Personality Inventory. While personality questionnaires offer the recruiter some useful information, it is important to note that personality tests have been known to produce 'socially desirable' responses (Rosse et al, 1998) in which responses are tweaked so that applicants present themselves in a more positive light. Overall, the predictive validity score of cognitive (0.63, Cook, 2009) and aptitude tests (0.55, Schmidt and Hunter, 1998) are considered robust.

In promoting fairness and in an attempt to predict future performance, assessment must measure what it is supposed to measure. The end result in the selection process is to determine the most important and critical aspects of the job, so that key attributes and evaluations can be fairly assessed for both existing and anticipated jobs. For potential employees this means recruitment and selection methods must be non-discriminatory: that is, no test must disadvantage any group on the basis of gender, culture or ethnicity. However, selection tests have been known to neglect the needs or traits of certain demographic groups in terms of ethnicity, disability, gender and age. For example, gender differences have been found with personality testing (Furnham, 2005). In measurement terms this is referred to as 'differential validity'; when an assessment predicts performance differently for different demographic groups, then the assessment is classified as an unfair selection practice (Ployhart and Holtz, 2008). Lastly, it is important to reiterate that while psychometric tests are standardized, their measures are far from perfect. For this reason it is thought that good practice is to combine different forms of selection.

Interviews

The employment interview is described by Eder and Harris (1999: 2) as:

> an interviewer–applicant exchange of information in which the
> interviewer inquire into the applicant's (a) work-related knowledge,
> skills and abilities (KSAs); (b) motivations; (c) values; and (d) reliability,
> with the overall staffing goals of attracting, selecting and retaining
> a highly competent and productive workforce.

The employment interview has three purposes. The first relates to the interviewer, who tries to evaluate, assess and makes a professional judgement about an applicant's suitability. The second is for the employer to sell the job. The third is directed to the interviewee, who is given the opportunity to exchange information about him/herself. The latter is of great significance; industry leaders we interviewed raised their concerns that many graduates arriving at interviews unprepared. To reiterate, a candidate may be deemed 'able' even though s/he performs poorly in the interview (ie comes across as unprepared); this judgement, however, is no guarantee of success in the workplace.

Interviews can be structured, unstructured or situational, and are generally carried out face to face, by phone or, most recently, over the internet. Structured interviews are the most standardized, because they prescribe predetermined questions and standardized rating protocols. This could explain their high predictive validity score of 0.63 (Cook, 2009), compared with unstructured interviews' score of 0.51 (Schmidt and Hunter, 1998) and situational validity score of 0.50 (Maurer, Sue-Chan and Latham, 1999). Some have, however, argued that this structure and rigidity does not allow applicants enough scope to showcase their unique attributes.

Unstructured interviews are said to have shortcomings too, due to their shorter duration as well as their informal and random questioning style (Campion, Palmer and Campion, 1997). This makes it difficult at times for applicants to give appropriate answers. In contrast, situational interviews are aimed at future-orientated situations; applicants are asked to envision what they would do in various hypothetical situations.

The behavioural structured interview, also referred to as the competency-based interview, is based on the assumption that past behaviour is the best indicator for predicting future behaviour (Latham and Sari, 1984). But what exactly are competencies? Competency-based theory gives rise to three models. The US model defines competency as 'an underlying characteristic of an individual in that it may be a motive, trait, skill, aspect of one's self-image or social role, or a body of knowledge that one uses' (Boyatzis, 1982: 41), whereas the UK model refers to competence as the 'skill and the standard of performance reached' (Rowe, 1995: 12). The third model of organizational competence talks about competency as 'a system that provides business capabilities to respond to internal and external stimuli' (Cruz-Cunha *et al*, 2011: 132).

It is said that competency-based interviews provide richer opportunities for interviewees to talk about their competencies, skills and previous work experience (Kessler, 2006). Many organizations favour the competency-based interview method because of its structured nature and questioning style. Questions are directed towards job-specific attributes that have been thoughtfully identified (if the interview is well planned) and measured against a stringent scoring matrix. There are a wide range of competencies (see Table 1.1) that applicants can be questioned about, with some more relevant than others depending on the criteria sets of the job on offer.

TABLE 1.1 Listing of competencies

Leadership	Relationship-building
Team work	Customer service
Problem-solving	Empathy
Communication	Analytical
Resilience	Organizational awareness
Flexibility	Time-management
Innovation	Developing others
Numerical	Written communication
Reflexivity	Willingness to learn
Open-mindedness	Achievement orientation
Conflict resolution	Self-control
Initiative	Computer literacy
Confidence	Directiveness
Commitment	Conceptual thinking
Adaptability	Order and planning

SOURCE: Adapted from Rainsbury *et al* (2002).

While the practice of competency-based interviewing attempts to unpack this through evidence-based examples, the selection process remains a challenge for recruiters in deciding who is fundamentally Mr or Ms Right. One method that supplements this process is the 'realistic job preview' (RJP). The rationale is to provide applicants with a more realistic view of their prospective roles. In doing so, candidates are presented with both positive and less positive job-related information about the organization and the job. If job (role) expectations are managed earlier on in the selection process this might attract the right pool of applicants, which in turn could reduce turnover. Furthermore, the RJP is particularly useful at the final stages of the selection process, as it assists applicants in their decision-making by enabling them to view the work on video, talk to existing job holders or have the opportunity to shadow them (Tate, 1994). In line with these ideas, Henrietta Lovell of the Rare Tea Company explains:

> we always ask new recruits to come in and actually do some work with us before we make a decision. It is often informal, to see what they are like. It gives us a picture of how they fit in and whether they are prepared to fit in. When you ask someone to do something, especially something small and seemingly unimportant, you can see his or her reaction. If they do not do it with good grace that is very telling.

Despite the wide range of opinions, interviewing, says Barclay (1999: 134), 'is still the most commonly used method of selection in employment, in spite of the fact that many studies have shown it to be a very flawed technique'. Some advocate its usefulness and claim interviews are more flexible and more cost-effective than alternative selection practices (eg assessment centres). This is particularly evident when dealing with smaller applicant numbers (Myers and Myers, 1980). Furthermore, the general consensus agrees that, despite concerns about predictive validity, structured interviews' scores are significantly more accurate than alternative selection methodologies.

Concerns have been raised about how interviewers process information and practise decision-making in trying to find the right candidate for the job. The ideal is that interviewers will show a high degree of professionalism and a wide range of attributes; in most cases however, interviewers are not always handed the appropriate techniques or tools, or are not well qualified to interview, as the following examples will illustrate.

Causal sense-making – interviewers

When interviewer and interviewee find themselves face to face, they engage in a two-way causal sense-making process (Anderson, 1992). These causal interactions are referred to as a 'conversation with a purpose', in which both interviewer and interviewee engage in a social interaction (Shackleton and Newell, 1997). For the interviewer, the process is about profiling and collating information. With that information, interviewers build a story that helps recruiters arrive at a decision. However, decision-making is often blurred as a result of information-processing errors. The following paragraphs will focus first on the causal sense-making practices of interviewers, and then on those of the interviewee.

To begin, barriers and information processing errors have been known to affect decision-making accuracy. For example, when interviewers are asked to validate the information in front of them that they use to reach selection decisions, they typically evaluate candidates' responses (Sandberg, 2013) rather than focusing on what candidates can do. Another influence on decision-making is the halo effect: if the applicant displays a particular behaviour type or trait in one single situation, the interviewer assumes that person will behave in the same way in other cases (Thorndike, 1920). Such assumptions create further glitches through the formation of interview bias, in which positive interviewee responses can lead to distorted perceptions. Levels of attractiveness are also known to influence the outcome of interviews, in that more attractive candidates are automatically assumed to be more effective than less attractive ones (Shahani, Dipboye and Gehrlein, 1993). Gender attribution bias also affects decision-making, with women often on the receiving end. According to Silvester and Chapman (1996), bias generates problems when candidates are questioned unfairly due to their gender. The authors claim that in interview situations women are more frequently than their male counterparts exposed to closed questions rather than open questions. This creates unfairness between the sexes as it does not give women the same opportunities to elaborate as their male candidates.

Other problems occur when interviewers fail to reach a joint consensus. Usually this is due to interviewers having different perceptions of candidates. This is also captured through Kelly's (1955: 55) construct of 'individuality corollary': that is, 'people differ from each other in their construction of events' – mainly, explains Kelly (1963: 120), because a 'person's processes are psychologically channelled by the ways in which he or she anticipates events'. Individuals use their own personal construct system (ie people develop their own meanings); that is what gives them their own individuality and distinct personhood (Jankowicz, 2004). For this reason, two people will always experience the 'same' situation differently, and understand and interpret it differently. Ideally, in an interview situation assessors must exercise a construct of 'commonality corollary', which is 'the extent that one person employs a construction of experience which is similar to that employed by another, his processes are psychologically similar to those of the other person' (Kelly, 1991: 90).

The psychology of perception claims that we select and interpret our surroundings in terms of a classification system or frame of reference (schema) already present in our own mind (Millar, Crute and Hargee, 1992). These predetermined schemas produce incongruences – that is, 'cognitive dissonance' – that are revealed in the feeling of discomfort experienced when we hold contradicting schemas (Festinger, 1954). In conserving our belief systems and ignoring the incongruency, distortions arise in how surroundings are interpreted. It is this incongruency that makes the selection interview vulnerable to biases – for example in the form of ethnocentrism, or when candidates are placed under scrutiny as a result of ethnocentric attributions. This manifests itself in stereotypical views that surface during the interview process where interviewers form biases of a cultural or gender-based nature (Silvester and Chapman, 1996).

Other explanations have been sought in trying to unpack individuals' decision-making processes. If interviewers do not collectively have a solid understanding of the required job criteria sets or do not identify the necessary answers that test these job sets, inconsistencies may lead to judgement errors. While clearly defined protocols are supposedly built in to diminish confusion, problems still arise. For example, when interviewers are randomly chosen to sit on an interview panel yet have no knowledge of the role or have minimum information about the candidate, this poses a problem. Of course, if other interview panellists are familiar with the job demands, this will prompt some level of quality assurance. The question remains, however: to what extent does this affect the overall selection-making process?

Causal sense-making – interviewees

The interviewee also engages in causal sense-making (Anderson, 1992). When examining interview situations more carefully, it is difficult not to see them as unnatural. Causal sense-making can serve as a useful tool for interviewees, as it helps structure their thoughts and decipher environmental cues. Interviewees who have the potential to spot cues will be in a better position to adjust their behaviours or answers. One method that helps to adjust behaviours is though the concept of 'matching and mirroring', a neuro-linguistic programming (NLP) technique known to help build rapport simply by matching one's communication style with that of the other person (Bandler, Fitzpatrick and Roberti, 2014). Following non-verbal cues can provide a useful measure for understanding others, regardless of the time constraints imposed on interview situations. Interestingly, Rosenthal and DePaulo (1979) claim that socially and emotionally savvy people have a greater ability to act on this because they know how to decode or scan for non-verbal and vocal cues, then use this information to adjust the way they respond.

In their studies of non-verbal communications, Mehrabian (1972) and Birdwhistell (1971) point out that non-verbal communication speaks louder than words. In fact, 55 per cent of non-verbal messages are transmitted through non-verbal signals in the form of facial expressions, gestures and mannerisms (Birdwhistell, 1971). The non-verbal message is also partially inferred through our vocal tone and 'voice'. Vocal characteristics account for 38 per cent of the impact of what is said; they include pitch variations (high, sharp, low or soothing sounds), tone/rate variations (harsh, smooth, even paced, slow or fast) and quality of breath (nasal, breathless, rich or clipped), while verbal communication – that is, the actual words spoken, used primarily to convey information – accounts for only 7 per cent of the received message. This affects the level of synchronicity between what a person says and how this fits with their non-verbal signalling of facial expressions, gestures and bodily mannerisms (see Chapter 4). People who are verbally in sync with what they say show physical congruence. To achieve this, individuals must above all be 'true'. Practising this takes courage according to spiritual teacher and author Eckhart Tolle (2001), who describes the journey of mind, body and learning towards being in the present, claiming it not only enhances greater self-awareness but equally makes individuals more receptive to their surroundings. The act of being present enables us to operate at a conscious level, which in turn makes it possible to tweak behaviour. Table 1.2 compiles a list of non-verbal cues to look out for, and their likely meanings.

Thus the potential errors made by interviewers in processing information place interviewees in a difficult situation, even forcing some to adjust their responses or behaviours in order to suit the interviewer or given context. The proposal here is that personality is fixed and cannot be linked with external behaviour. Thus, in trying to make sense of behaviour, cues are drawn from non-verbal behaviour (eg observing eye contact) and conclusions made about the underlying personality. This makes the selection practice an awkward one, since the concept of personality makes it difficult for assessors to predict how potential recruits will behave in a given situation.

The last potential decision-making error made by interviewers can be explained through the Similarity–Attraction Paradigm. This theory affirms that similarity in attitude, belief, education or background (Berger, 1952; Newcomb, 1956; Shaw, 1971) is at the root of attraction (eg Newcomb, 1956; Rosenbaum, 1986). Originally formulated by Tajfel (1979) and Turner (1996), and in close alignment to the above, Social Identity theory explains the dynamics of in-group behaviour. Groups develop social identities. The reason for this, Turner explains, is that individuals by default have a psychological need to belong to a distinct group. As a result, individuals react more favourably to those who are similar; thus, in interview situations, interviewers

TABLE 1.2 Indicators of non-verbal cues

Non-verbal cue	Possible meaning
Two raised eyebrows, enlarged pupils, sudden attention directed at speaker	Surprise
Eyes directed to ceiling, blinking rapidly, turning away and looking steadily into the air, walking back and forth	Decision-making in progress
Deep breath and sigh followed by relaxation, end of facial tension, smiling or earnest eye contact	Decision has been made
Arms open, high level of eye contact, whilst offering new information	Consensus building
Pregnant pause without negative gestures	Seeking more information
Change of pitch or tone of voice	Repositioning of thought process or impression
Keeps on periphery, waits for others to initiate contact, curling shoulders forward, seeking approval, looking down	Feeling of subordinate status. Internal dialogue
Eyes looking down, low energy, poor responsiveness	Trying to understand or interpret information
Nodding, smiling, relaxation following concentration, relaxed eye contact, crossing legs towards speaker, matching body movements and positions	Agreement, approval
Quietly spoken, non-defensive	Open to behaviour, seeking to move forward
Even breathing, arms folded loosely, leaning forward, good eye contact	Interest, receptiveness
Too much eye contact	Excitement, expectancy, feeling of empathy
Eye contact, smiling, enlarged pupils, relaxed open posture, serene, facial expression free unrestrained movement	Happiness, satisfaction, common ground

SOURCE: Walkley Associates (c) NLP and Assessment Practitioner.

will make assumptions based on in and out-group memberships. By default, they will respond positively to candidates they perceive as similar (eg in gender, culture, background) while attributing negative characteristics to those seen as dissimilar, even when the interviewer believes the candidate is suitable (Anderson, 1992).

On a larger scale, the so-called similarity effect (Fisher, 1994), warns Bennis (1998), means jobs offered to candidates similar in mindset, educational attainment and background, which can put organizations at risk of creating a working population that is a group of clones. While some degree of homogeneity is of course important, Bennis remains wary of the so-called '*doppelganger* (double) effect', suggesting excess cloning not only inhibits innovation but can also lead to stagnation. Moreover, too much similarity will cause groupthink and conformity (see Chapter 4) and, surprisingly, even set the scene for workplace romances. The latter idea casts a novel light on the selection process and leaves one wondering whether organizations could be unwittingly responsible for creating the perfect playground for romance.

In a recent survey by CareerBuilder.co.uk (2014) of 1,000 full-time workers across different UK industries, it was found that 39 per cent had had intimate relationships with a co-worker, while 16 per cent repeatedly did so. If organizations are recruiting based on type, could this hold the key to the ongoing recurrence of workplace romances? According to Gautier (2007), this may well be the case. Inherent in the recruitment and selection process is identification of the candidates' values, beliefs or interests and whether these match the culture of the given organization. In addition, when shared similarities, as described in the Similarity-Attraction Paradigm (Newcomb, 1956), are combined with the Mere Exposure Effect (Zajonc, 1968) as well as an increase in organizational demands (eg longer working hours), it is no surprise, then, that intimate relationships flourish, making workplace romances inherently become part of organizational life.

The workplace romance phenomenon raises an interesting debate, with some accepting that is often a part of working life; as Chris Butt, CEO of Cognisess, says:

it is inevitable – people, passion and all the things that create a romance... increasingly we are spending more time at work than at home so you create bonds and attractions. It is a human scenario and it would be unwise for corporations to have a policy.

Others argued against it, including notary public Riccardo Genghini, of Studio Notarile Genghini & Associati, who affirms: 'I discourage them [affairs].' When organizations do opt to prohibit workplace romances, it is usually under the pretext that such relations trigger either favouritism (Quinn, 1977) or loss of productivity (Pierce, Byrne and Aguinis, 1996). As former General Manager of North American Operations at Voith Industrial Services Inc Linda DeGrow explains: 'when there is any type of a reporting relationship, or a situation where a quid pro quo can exist, romance in those situations is not a good practice.' Along similar lines, HR Director Simon Lloyd, of Santander comments: 'it must be ensured that this does not interfere with the running of the organization either from a control point of view or from a performance point of view.'

On the other hand, Gautier (2007) found that when people are involved in a workplace romance they are happier in their work, and Devine and Markiewicz (1990) and Pierce (1998) reported an increase in performance levels. One suggested reason for the increase in performance levels is that romantic couples are more eager to impress superiors due to a fear of stigma (Pierce and Aguinis, 2003; Powell and Foley, 1998). As the controversy among scholars and industry leaders interviewed for this book shows, opinions vary as to the rights and wrongs of workplace romances. Perhaps the central concern for organizations should be not to thwart relations, but rather to instil a sense of decorum in the workplace, since there is no clear indication these relations will cease.

References

References are used during the third and final stage of the selection process. They usually serve as a final check before the job is offered. According to Shackleton and Newell (1997), references have a range of purposes. For example, they are used as a check to ascertain the accuracy of information provided by the applicant, or to collate information about the applicant's prior employment history and performance. Referencing formats range from open-ended enquiries to structured ones with questions directly related to the job criteria.

Similarly, writing references, says Doyle (2003), can cause difficulty for referees, particularly where applicants have held a different role from the one on offer, even when skills are transferable. Furthermore, third-party opinions are not always considered reliable – after all, who would be willing to write a negative reference? Recruiters continue to turn a blind eye to the well-documented low predictive validity scores of 0.26 (see for example Cook, 2009) and low criterion-related and inter-rated reliability scores (eg Smith and Smith, 2005). Catano (2012), however, argues that when multiple references are used, this can improve validity scores as it limits the potential for respondent bias to invalidate the reference. Despite their imperfections, references continue to be used, most commonly in the UK, Ireland and Belgium, followed by France, Sweden, The Netherlands and Portugal (Shackleton and Newell, 1997).

Conclusion

In this chapter the historical foundations of work have been described and how the discipline of work psychology evolved. Despite the revolutionary breakthrough of the Hawthorne studies, it is still questionable whether today's working practices mirror the ideas advocated by Elton Mayo. Advances in the studies of organizational psychology have led to the process of job analysis. If conducted thoroughly, the analysis will lead to clearly prescribed job descriptions and person specifications. A number of standardized selection tests are available to help find the right candidates. Despite claims of predictive validity for many of these tests, their results are far from perfect. It is therefore best to use a mixture of methodological practices to allay concerns about test validity.

Without question, the role that SHRM plays in encouraging organizational visionary planning is pivotal in the management of human capital. Yet, equally important is to consider how this may be achieved.

It would require a shift in mindset in the decisions that organizations make about people, and even the type of applicants they may be looking for. Chapter 2 will now examine what employers are drawn to and how those currently in search of work can improve their chances of being selected.

Employability

02

This chapter explores ideas about employment opportunities, with a focus on employability. It will provide some answers to the question of why many graduates are forced to apply for jobs outside their field of expertise, and other considerations that may affect tenure. For example, what is the role of education and how can it contribute towards employability? The discussion will then aim to identify what organizations need from workers to be successful in the current climate, and what the demands are on workers to survive and cope with the challenges of today's workplace. Ideas will evolve from the thoughts of the industry leaders interviewed for this book. To begin with, we need to consider what employability is.

What is employability?

Employability is considered to be 'the skills, knowledge, technology and adaptability to enable [people] to enter and remain in employment throughout their working lives' (HM Treasury, 1997: 1). The Dearing Report further suggests that employability revolves around communication, information technology (IT) and openness to learning (NCIHE, 1997). Other important skill sets include the jobholder's ability to self-manage, self-motivate, be organized, work in teams and show commitment (Hillage and Pollard, 1998). With recent changes in customer service industries, new employability skill sets have become important: customer and business awareness (CBI, 2007: 12) and problem-solving skills (UKCES, 2009: 10–11). Contrary to the general belief, employability does not include the fundamentals of basic numeracy and literacy skills, one's specialized subject degree area (Belt, Drake and Chapman, 2010) or the acquisition of a job. Rather, employability has two aspects that relate to workers already in employment and those who are actively looking for work. The former are preoccupied with career development, in which workers show scope for growth and development opportunities. For the individual, this means that those who develop additional skills in their current roles become more valuable, which places them in a stronger position to move into better or new roles.

Graduate employment

The general consensus on graduate employment is that higher education is critical for economic prosperity and social mobility. Since 1990 the United Kingdom has witnessed a huge increase in the number of graduates (ONS, 2012a); in 2013 the figure stood at 12 million (ONS, 2013). Yet many struggle to secure employment, or end up in non-graduate jobs (HECSU, 2012).

In 2012, leading UK employers recruited fewer graduates than in previous years, reducing their graduate intake by more than 1,200 (ONS, 2012a). Compared to the recruitment figures of 2011, entry-level vacancies decreased by 0.8 per cent in 2012 (High Fliers, 2013). Reductions in vacancies were witnessed across a range of sectors including accounting, professional services industries and banking. On the other hand, some sectors have compensated for the entry-level shortfall: sectors such as the public sector, engineering and industrial companies and retail (High Fliers, 2013).

The current situation in graduate employment suggests that it is proving harder and harder for students to establish themselves in work (ONS, 2012c). The graduates who are more successful in obtaining work in their chosen fields are often those who have achieved very good classes of degrees (HECSU, 2012). The result is that many graduates have been forced to apply for jobs outside their field of expertise – usually not from choice, but because they have been unsuccessful in their chosen subject area – with the result that they end up taking on lower-paid or temporary work (High Fliers, 2013). This creates a knock-on effect not only for those who are have qualifications but also for those at the bottom of the educational pyramid. Both of these parties are now in direct competition for lower-skilled jobs.

This also raises important questions about the mix of skills required and the choices students are making, which can pose a difficult dilemma: should students select courses on the basis of market skill shortages or should they choose them on the basis of their personal interests?

Interviews with students revealed differing motivations in their choice of degree. Some make the choice due to intrinsically driven motivation: that is, their choices are based solely on their desires. For example, one 22-year-old female student interviewed said: 'I took the course first because of my interest in the field and the different career options available, and second to pursue a professional career.' For others the choice of degree is driven extrinsically: that is by rewards and/or external outcomes. This is highlighted by the response of a 23-year-old male psychology student who we interviewed: 'It seemed essential; everyone has it nowadays.' Other reasons can also be important. A 21-year-old female psychology student revealed that: 'It was my family who wanted me to have a degree and pushed me in my education.'

There may even be doubts as to whether the higher education route is the right choice at all. Upon reflection, this third-year student says: 'I would have maybe looked more into apprenticeship schemes.' This raises the question whether enough is being done to promote other educational and/or alternative routes. Despite the funding of more than 250,000 apprenticeships since 2011 and a recent bid offering 3,000 training internships as part of a £37 million government incentive to the creative industry, the current situation indicates that more needs to be done to develop employment options for graduates and school leavers.

In contrast to these comments, Jon Hall, former rugby player for Bath, says that there is a need for greater determination and confidence when choosing a career path. To do so, the current managing director of PGIR Limited clarifies, it is helpful to 'ask yourself what business you want to be in and what you want from your career. Once you have chosen an area, understand where you can go with it.' Similarly Louise Hill, former assistant general manager at Gaucho, explains:

'Just find what it is that you love and do it to your best ability. Don't compromise;, you'll be doing it for a long time so it's better that you do it well and enjoy it.' For this reason, affirms PhD candidate and teaching assistant Michael Aldous of the LSE: 'Take as many opportunities as you possibly can to do different things. I think that will give you a broad range of experiences that will help you to really think what you want to do as you go through your career.' Michael's final thought leads nicely into the final employability problem discussed in this chapter.

A third challenge that concerns employment is work experience. Many graduate programmes and/or vacancies tend to be filled by those who were lucky enough to have been exposed to work experience earlier on during their degree courses (ONS, 2012c). Perhaps this explains why some learning institutions, including the University of Westminster, are keen to offer undergraduate psychology students an extra-curricular year-long placement. By exposing them to workplace settings, the 'learning-by-doing' experience enhances the students' employability. This practice is also not unusual in graduate programme settings, not least in the fields of organizational and clinical psychology where courses are built around work placements.

Some organizations however are, are prepared to take on inexperienced recruits as Santander's Human Resource Director, Simon Lloyd, affirms: 'Work experience is not a requirement' (though he notes that: 'We do find that it gives candidates an advantage in replying to competency-based questions.') Similarly, university reader Samantha Faro says: 'Most of us begin our academic careers with no prior teaching experience. Providing you receive the right support you can develop your teaching experience.'

Some argue that when candidates enter as a 'blank canvas' – that is, free of 'employment baggage'; this makes them easier to mould as they have no previous work experience to compare with their new employer. This is not a negative; indeed it makes the training process more manageable as recruits can be easily directed towards the organizations' ethos. This is good news for graduates who have no or little experience. Nonetheless, Ward Edmonds, manager at TrateMedia JLT in the United Arab Emirates, recommends: 'If you have the choice, go for experience above income to begin with. Go for a company that will nurture you rather than simply pay you.' Likewise, department manager Roland Esnis at IBM advises: 'Develop experience rather than aim for specific job roles.'

These comments suggest that, in a bid to improve graduate employment prospects, two measures are needed: the first is to reiterate the importance of employability and the role of education, and the second is to re-address the employability skill sets that employers want.

What do employers seek?

The Association of Graduate Recruiters suggest that graduates from higher education sometimes lack the necessary employability skills for the roles they aspire to. Many of the 750 employers represented by the association claim that graduates often fail to meet even the basic job requirements and standards expected of them (AGR, 2011). It seems recruiters are not alone in thinking graduates are ill equipped with basic employability skills. For example, though 68 per cent of the employers surveyed by the Institute of Directors (2007) felt their graduates knew their subjects reasonably well, 45 per cent were dissatisfied with graduates' generic employability skill sets, citing a lack of business awareness, self-management skills and communication.

Employers also felt that a mere 25 per cent of graduates and non-graduates were thoroughly prepared for employment, while 40 per cent of graduates did not demonstrate the necessary abilities (CBI and UUK, 2009). In exploring the reasons for this lack of preparedness, 103 third-year undergraduates were asked to complete a questionnaire consisting of four closed and six open-ended questions. To the question, 'Has your degree sufficiently prepared you for the world of work?' 66 per cent of the 103 students answered that their degree had prepared them for employability, while 33 per cent did not think this was the case. The data obtained from students who felt that their degree had sufficiently prepared them for the world of work were categorized into three classes (see Table 2.1). (Some of these were in alignment with the competencies listed by Rainsbury *et al* (2002) and shown in Table 1.1 in the previous chapter.)

TABLE 2.1   Employability skill sets acquired through the degree
course (N = 103)

Academic	Behavioural	Tools
Critical thinking	Communication	Presentations
Writing	Collaboration	Time management
Analytical	Empathy	Conferences
Brain function	Achievement orientation	Professionalism
Theory	Self-control	Organizational
Psychometrics	Open-minded	Planning
Understanding	Assertiveness	Debating
EEG function	Relationship building	Proposal writing
Ethics	Respect	Reports
SPSS	Motivation	Recruitment
Questioning	Listening	Personality questionnaires
Vocabulary	Confidence	Poster design

The first category refers to skills of an academic nature. Students report here proficiency in, for example, their 'ability to think and write professionally, research skills and analysis' (female, 30, law). In the behavioural element that forms the second category, students refer to changes in their attitudes. For example, one student explains how she learnt to work better with others by being more 'patient, empathetic and understanding of others' (female, 22, psychology). Others stated they had become more confident: 'I feel I have gained personal confidence and interpersonal skills as well as a broader mind and a better understanding of the world' (female, 20, psychology and sociology). The third category consists of development tools. Here students accumulated generic skills varying from time management and planning skills to adapting to different situations, organizing and working as a team.

The 33 per cent of students who felt that their degree did not prepare them well for the world of work, expressed a number of reasons for their feelings. For example, one 21-year-old female psychology student felt that 'although it provides a lot of useful and essential theory it would be useful to provide some practical skills that can be transferred into the workplace'. Another psychology student affirmed that 'the degree has given me enough knowledge and skill to present myself as a whole and understand aspects of psychology in itself; however it has not given a worldwide or real-life perspective. There have been very few opportunities to see real-life applications of our modules and there have not been a lot of productive outsiders giving professional experience and pathway opportunities to students. Out of my six modules, only one provided me with this' (female, 21).

What is interesting here is that these findings suggest two possible reasons for the lack of preparedness. Educators might be failing (some) students in the matter of employability, as pointed out by one female psychology and criminology student who says: 'I think graduates should be told more about employability opportunities, which should be available and relevant to their course.' Or the message is conveyed clearly yet these students are simply not able to connect the dots. What this information suggests is that degree courses do not necessarily correlate with real-life employability skill sets. It is thought that perhaps better links could be made in an attempt to fill these gaps. Perhaps, industry leaders should be granted greater access to courses to walk students through real-life anecdotes that relate to working life. Industry leader Hugo Chapman, Head of the Department of Prints and Drawings at the British Museum, illustrates this well by explaining how: 'In my world being able to write fluently and put your arguments succinctly, to persuade someone to lend their collection or whatever, is important.' As well as communication, Hugo stipulates that being able to get on with people, is also crucial. One way to develop succinct writing skills is through the practice of essay writing. Yet, as one 20-year-old student (female, psychology and sociology) observed 'I feel university teaches you how to answer an exam question or essay, not how to use these skills in the workplace', suggesting no clear links have been made here.

Several explanations are given as to why this may be. For a start, with more pressure for graduates to do well, it is no surprise that many feel the urge to focus on results rather than the learning process. As this 21-year-old female student highlights: 'I believe there is very intense competition for psychology positions; this I am worried about.' Controversial, though worthy of exploration, is to consider the current factors that drive students. Could it be that universities are creating learning environments that are unwittingly steering students towards performance and marks? Oddly enough, these perceptions also appeared in the data sets, in which one student observed: 'There is too much emphasis on marks and too many assessments with few links to the workplace' (male, 24, psychology). Also, 'I am in my final year, and really I am being strategic in the modules I choose, only because I know I will get good grades. Without these grades, I probably won't get ahead or will end up in a low-status job.' Industry leader Guy Kendall, former systems engineer at the National Theatre, argues against this viewpoint by saying that to 'be genuine and truthful and seek the challenges that stretch your ability rather than only doing what you think you can achieve' is inherent to the learning and development process. Guy adds: 'Key to employability is not to be afraid of failure but to learn from your mistakes, never stop learning, never stop trying to find out more about the bigger picture, and not to view your career in isolation but rather see how all the pieces fit together.' Reich (2002) describes this vision particularly well through a four-dimensional taxonomy:

- *system thinking*, which is about understanding the bigger picture;
- *abstraction*, which involves learning how to apply theories, models and formulae;
- *experimentation*, which develops intuition as well as analytical development;
- *collaboration*.

Reich's Taxonomy Model nicely suggests how learning and employment may be related, forming a so-called life cycle of the two. It seems that when some parts of this cycle are missing, that's when the challenges occur. For example, development of collaborative ability entails learning how to work with others, which is best practised through group work. Emphasizing group work while studying for a degree may well help students to develop this ability and improve their confidence in working with others. Building confidence is also about managing mistakes, taking accountability for our mistakes, and above all says Evanita ten Napel, who works in credit sales at Mitsubishi UFJ Securities International, 'not taking anything personally, especially when mistakes are made'. Effectively, what employers seek, explains Isabelle Minneci, Human Resource Director at L'Oréal, are candidates who 'always try to learn and develop from others'. Inherent to this development process is to respect experience and to learn that sometimes others are better than you. The key says Qantas Chief Marketing Officer Lewis Pullen is 'not to be intimidated by this'.

Different types of studies recognize that different types of employment require a multitude of employability skill sets. With that in mind, perhaps now would be the appropriate moment to end the discussion of employability and (through the data sets) consider what employers actually consider important competencies. Thus let us consider the question: what do employers seek in potential recruits? Interestingly, the data revealed that similar skill sets were widely required among the employers interviewed (see Table 2.2).

Linda DeGrow, former general manager at Voith Industrial Services Inc, looks for graduates who 'exhibit specific competencies/behaviours. Standard behaviours expected would include self-responsibility, continuous learning, initiative, emotional composure and goal orientation.' BBC broadcaster and journalist Sian Williams insists workers must have 'good team skills, punctuality, high ethical and moral standards, work hard, be nice, support others, come up with ideas, give more than they expect, admit your mistakes, help colleagues through theirs. Be calm in a crisis, earn the respect of those you work with and show them the respect they deserve.'

TABLE 2.2   Job-related competencies extracted from industry leaders (N = 32)

Passion	Hunger	Integrity
Communication	Modesty	Team worker
Creativity	Decisiveness	Flexibility
Resilience	Honesty	Ethical/moral standards
Punctuality	Ambition	Conflict resolution
Planning	Go the extra mile	Responsibility
Drive	Action	Motivation
Enthusiasm	Selling	Innovative
Humility	Influence	Initiative
Professionalism	Listening	Trustworthy
Self-respect	Kindness	Fairness
Relationship building	Empathy	Sociability
Good nature	Friendly	Willingness to learn
Intelligence	Cognition	Self-control
Mobility	Resourceful	Respect for others
Specialization	Commitment	Entrepreneurial

Interestingly, although the majority of employers who were interviewed for this book emphasized that theoretical knowledge is important, they agree that it is not the deciding factor in recruitment. Other employability skill sets seem to carry more weight. Maike van der Hooghen, who works as Head of Branch at the Ministry of Defence in the Netherlands, affirms: 'I would rather have someone who is able to handle disappointments and bounces back, than someone with the right academic background.' For Henrietta Lovell, founder of the Rare Tea Company, her preferred candidate is:

[someone] with energy and drive. I need them to innovate and be creative, to come up with ideas about how to change things and have ideas about new business. I do not want people who just want to come in and do a job. They have to believe that what we are doing really matters – that we can cause a revolution. They really have to be hopeful and say: 'even though this is not the way the world is, it could be.'

Shai Greenberg at boutique salon Gielly Green's recruitment motto is 'honesty', and Shai adds:

Be yourself. It may be good for you or bad, but you cannot play a game for a long time. Some people come in and say something amazing and after two months you can see right through them and so on. The worst mistake is to keep someone who is not committed to the business, so you give someone three months and you find out how they get on, how they connect with the business.

Also a strong advocate for the 'honesty' trait is Professor of Surgery Guy Samama, formerly employed as Head of Department at Caen University Hospital.

Another important employability quality that industry leaders seek is the candidate's willingness to start at the bottom. Most of the respondent mentioned this, though some disagreed, claiming graduates are not always prepared to start on the ground floor. Some of the students highlighted reasons they felt reluctant to do so. For example: 'Because I feel that with my motivation, current achievement and goals I have an advantage over (some) other individuals and if I'm not challenged enough I will get bored' (female, 25, psychology). One student asked: 'Why should I start at the bottom if I am qualified?' (female, 22, PR/advertising). Another commented that 'I'd be prepared to start somewhere in the middle' (male, psychology and sociology), while one was adamant that 'People with a degree should not have to work from the bottom' (female, 22, psychology).

Industry leader Guy Lootens, general manager of Novotel in Belgium, finds this behaviour type incomprehensible and says: 'More and more graduates want to come straight out of the school and start as managers. They complete their studies and have their diploma so they say to themselves, "I can go for a manager's job".' He gives the example of a recruit who had graduated three months earlier and, when told he would have to start as a trainee, indignantly rejected the idea. 'Trainee?... No, I want to be on the front desk!' That implied he would not only be supervising the reception area but also responsible for liaising with housekeeping, food and beverage, the bar and other departments involved in caring for the guests. Guy replied that was not going to happen. The recruit would have to work as a trainee in each department, learning what the work involved and how they worked together, before he could take on a full front desk role. Guy is clear that: 'You have to start from the bottom, yes.'

Borja Manchado, resort manager at the Four Seasons Hotel, agrees. Many of his recruits have studied at some of the best schools in the world, but to succeed in the hospitality industry they have to get on with people and learn to deal with them. 'For that they need to start from the bottom and they need to be patient, because this is a long career and things don't happen overnight.' Before they can lead, they need experience of different situations and of the different cultures that will influence the behaviour of the people they have to work with.

These two managers confirm that newly qualified graduates are sometimes reluctant to start their career at the bottom. There is a gulf between the expectations of employers and graduates.

What other concerns do graduates have that contribute towards their unwillingness to start at the bottom? Hugo Chapman, a head of department at the British Museum, answers: 'The time factor... Everything is becoming hurried and fractured and moving from one project to another... it is more difficult to build up that kind of expertise.' This urgency does create problems for graduates and employers. Chapman sums it up very well by adding: 'You have to really want to do it, as I really did a lot of it in my own time. I did it because I was hungry for the knowledge. I wanted to find out and know more about it.' Similarly, industry leader Didier Souillat at Hakkasan notes that: 'Nothing comes free: you have to show willingness; you have to be hungry.' The managing director adds: 'After all, whom am I going to notice? I am going to notice the person who wants to be noticed, who shows hunger, who shows action, who communicates.' Yet sometimes, says Maike van der Hooghen:

> new recruits, when young, are too ambitious and cannot wait to get ahead – they forget they have to prove themselves first. They have to put in the hours, gain experience in all aspects of their work. If they do that, they will make a reputation for themselves as they proceed and they will get noticed.

This sense of haste is also expressed by Simon Lloyd, HR Director of Santander UK Plc, who said: 'Do not try to change the world immediately, do not burn yourself out; learn, do not decide immediately what you are going to do.'

There is a consensus that graduates should never stop listening and learning from others and should be open to start at the bottom. Simon Lloyd, HR director of Santander UK, notices difference between generations: 'Young people particularly have different views of the world and what they want to achieve. They prefer to be able to choose how they do things. They've grown up in a different era and therefore they have different approaches to life.' Basically, explains Didier Souillat, managing director at Hakkasan: 'The new generation is not very hungry.' These comments from industry leaders suggest that there are generational differences in attitudes to work, and that attitudes to work affect employability. We will return to the subject of generational differences in Chapter 7.

What all these findings also reveal is that, although the industry leaders interviewed come from varied sectors and backgrounds, they all identified similar sets of 'generic skills' as being key to employability and offer similar advice, with some emphasizing that monetary incentive should not be the sole determinant. Many also agree that, in order to find the right job, people must feel hungry for their vocational choice, though this may take some time to develop.

The real message however is that if we truly want to develop a nation of well-equipped, rounded and forward-thinking individuals, then graduates must be steered towards the right mindset since the majority, at some point in their career, will end up working in teams or in leadership roles. In developing the right mindset Dave Coplin, Chief Envisioning Officer at Microsoft, suggests the prime need is to

be mindful of the overall direction of travel, be respectful of the
environment that you are in. It does not matter if you are at the
beginning or end of your career. Open your eyes, and see and hear
things and understand and try not to fall into that mindset where
you do not see things around you or you cannot take that step back.

This, however, may well go beyond the employability calling and requires a whole new set of skills: the development of self-awareness
and presence. Only then does it become possible to be mindful of
what we do, how we do it and to whom.

Key to developing employment skills are the educators who design
curriculums and teaching. Perhaps, alongside educators, more partnerships are needed between industry leaders and academics. These
would help learners connect the dots and better understand the links
between theory and applied working knowledge.

Conclusion

This chapter has provided an analysis of what constitutes employability
and how this influences employment, and have given an overview of
the main selection methods used in recruitment and selection practices.
From a human capital viewpoint, organizations will be keen to
recruit candidates who not only have the capacity to function in a
given job but also exhibit a string of other employability skills. With
a particular focus on graduate employment, industry leaders say they
are drawn to candidates who possess the right attitude and relevant
traits to help drive their businesses forward. Important trait sets
include openness, flexibility, willingness to learn, resilience, passion
and hunger. Other findings from the research data suggest that degree
courses do not always clearly apply theoretical knowledge to real-life
working practices. Perhaps better links could be made in an attempt
to fill these gaps through more partnerships between industry leaders
and curriculum designers.

To close, the chapter has identified what it is that organizations
need from their workers to succeed in the current climate. With this
in mind, Chapter 3 will now explore theories of team development,
with a focus on building collaborative and sustainable teams.

Teams

03

Chapter 2 emphasized that for organizations to run successfully they must recruit people who fit their style of operation. The recruit will, in some shape or form, add value to the organization, along with a unique set of skills, whether functional or behavioural. An important aspect of the employability portfolio is the employee's capacity to work as part of a team. Since teamwork is considered an important aspect of organizational effectiveness, this chapter introduces the concept of team theories and the stages through which teams develop. Most theories suggest five phases; these include Tuckman and Jensen's Stages of Development (1977), Tjosvold's (1991) Team Organization Model) and Lacoursiere's Life Cycle of Stages (1980). A number of other theories propose a four-stage process: Hare's (1976) Functional Approach and Dyer, Dyer and Dyer's (2007) model of Four Cs. Unusually, the Punctuated Equilibrium Model (Gersick, 1988) does not incorporate a stage approach. The aim of this chapter is to raise awareness of ways to improve teamworking practices by reference to a variety of approaches. We begin with a brief overview of the prevalence and trends of teamwork in the UK and elsewhere, then look at the existing types of groups and teams.

In most Western European countries (eg The Netherlands, Denmark, Sweden) there has been a long tradition of teamwork, and upward trends can now be seen among former Eastern European nations (see Figure 3.1). A survey by the European Foundation for the Improvement of Living and Working Conditions showed countries such as Estonia and Bulgaria reaching record highs of 81 per cent and 67 per cent. In the UK and Ireland the levels were 80.6 per cent and 76 per cent, respectively (and 80.1 per cent in Malta) (EWCS, 2007).

FIGURE 3.1   Teamwork incidences in EU (%)

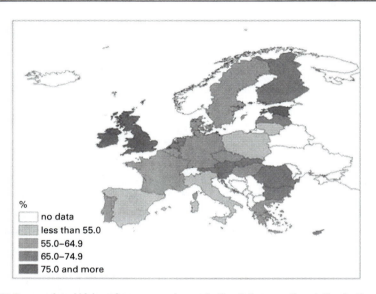

%
- no data
- less than 55.0
- 55.0–64.9
- 65.0–74.9
- 75.0 and more

SOURCE: Teamwork and high performance work organization © European Foundation for the improvement of Living and Working Conditions, 2007, Wyattville Road, Dublin, 18, Ireland, **www.eurofound.europe.eu**.

These increases are said to be the result of political changes and the expansion of the European Union, as well as changes in working methods. The lowest incidences of teamwork were found in Lithuania and Italy, at 38.3 per cent and 40.9 per cent; in Spain the average was 53.9 per cent and in Poland 54.3 per cent. Outside Europe, the team-based approach was seen in 87 per cent of companies in the United States (Robbins, 2001) and 45 per cent of those in Canada (Leckie *et al*, 2001). The survey also captured national differences in gender distribution, with Sweden, Ireland, Denmark and The Netherlands providing a more balanced picture of women and men working in teams compared with their EU partners of Poland, Portugal, Greece and Austria. This may be due to stronger gender segregation practices in certain sectors of these economies, where women are less represented. Due to the differences in cultural and historical backgrounds, it may be that in these countries organizational structures have given women less opportunity for employment and/or promotion. This in turn would lead to vertical as well as occupational segregation (Preston, 1999).

FIGURE 3.2   Teamwork incidence by occupation (%)

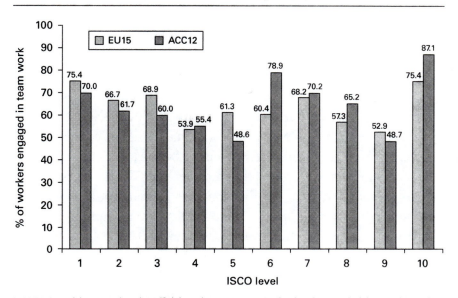

NOTES: 1. Legislators and senior officials and managers; 2. Professionals; 3. Technicians and associate professional; 4. Clerks; 5. Services workers and sales workers; 6. Skilled agricultural and fishery workers; 7. Craft and related trades workers; 8. Plant and machine operators and assemblers; 9. Elementary occupational; 10. Armed forces.

SOURCE: Teamwork and high performance work organization © European Foundation for the improvement of Living and Working Conditions, 2007, Wyattville Road, Dublin, 18, Ireland **www.eurofound.europe.eu**

Figure 3.2 gives a breakdown of the different occupational categories in which teamwork is carried out. It shows that the EU countries are typified by a predominance of teamwork among legislators, senior officials and managers (75.4 per cent), professionals (66.7 per cent) and technicians and associate professionals (68.9 per cent). Relatively high incidence rates can also be found among craft and related 'trades workers' (68.2 per cent), with lower incidences among plant and machine operators and assemblers (57.3 per cent), clerks (53.9 per cent), and unskilled workers (52.9 per cent) (EWCS, 2007: 14)

These findings indicate that clerks and assembly line operators have less interaction with other workers than professionals or skilled workers. While professionals and skilled workers carry out their work independently, they are also required to work horizontally – that is, in close coordination with other workers – to reach their overall goal.

Groups and teams

The terms 'group' and 'team' are often used interchangeably, yet the two are properly considered as separate entities. At first glance, the concepts seem indistinguishable yet subtle differences do exist: namely, in how they are formed and in their functionality. Shaver (1977: 557), for example, perceives groups as 'a collectivity that has psychological implications for the individual, based upon the person's awareness of other group members, his or her membership (or desired membership) in the group, and the emotional significance of the group'. Teams, in contrast, are typically defined as a 'small number of people with complementary skills who are committed to a common purpose, performing goals, and approach, for which they hold themselves mutually accountable' (Clutterbuck, 2007: 7).

Let us begin with groups. They can be categorized as primary and secondary, or formal and informal. Primary groups are defined by their size and degree of relationship. Compared with secondary groups, they are smaller, more communicative and more intimate, with a focus on building longer-lasting relations. Formal groups are clearly defined by the organization's structure, and for this reason governed by processes and regulations. They are generally designed to have a direct impact on the organization's collective purpose. They can be broken down into different types: command groups (eg boards of directors and committees), task groups (eg commissions) and project-based groups or ad-hoc committee groups.

FIGURE 3.3   Formal groups

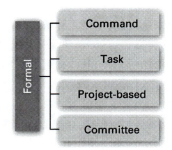

Command groups are best described as groups of people who come together on the basis of their seniority and positions in the organization. Individuals here will be high up in the chain of command, with authority and freedom to make decisions. For example, a head of department directly responsible for his/her staff would be seen as a command group member. Task groups, on the other hand, are made up of people drawn from across the organization, regardless of rank. Rather they are grouped together because of their particular skill sets and/or areas of expertise. Project-based groups are comparable to task groups, but are less permanent: they may be disbanded when projects are completed. Committees may be either permanent or temporary depending on their function.

What differentiates formal groups from informal groups is that membership of an informal group is voluntary. Individuals join because they want a sense of belonging. To help explain this process, in social psychology, the 'mere-exposure' effect (Zajonc, 1968) reveals how individuals naturally gravitate to one another: social relationships begin to develop and informal groups evolve (see Figure 3.4).

Informal groups thus grow out of shared identities and interests or develop through friendships. Sport clubs, interest groups, social networks and local community groupings are examples of informal groups. It must be noted that, while informal groups can enhance community, they are occasionally guilty of breeding cliques. Since clique-related behaviours tend to be associated with groupthink (Janis, 1972) and conformity (Asch, 1952; Sherif, 1936) – as discussed in Chapter 4 – they are likely to drive some members away. One way to manage cliques was suggested by Gaucho's former Assistant General Manager Louise Hill, who advises: 'Focus on the positive

FIGURE 3.4   Informal groups

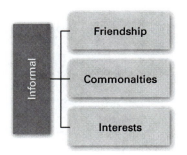

attributes, manage cliques and standards and don't allow [cliques] to exist.' In doing so, she suggests having 'regular meetings/briefings; this will bring team cohesion and a sense of camaraderie'. Above all: 'Manage behaviour and judge all members by the same criteria, regardless of whether they are your favourite or least favourite.'

Moving on to teams: work teams are composed of interdependent individuals who share responsibility for the overall outcomes of their work. They have different forms, and include problem-solving, cross-functional, self-directed, decision-making and global teams (see Figure 3.5).

Problem-solving teams are often created on an interim basis to concentrate on a specific task, while cross-functional teams are composed of individuals from differing departments or work areas that come together on a task, problem or project basis. Self-directed work teams generally consist of 10 to 15 members and are composed of experts. Their members for the most part operate autonomously, though provisions are in place that permit them to monitor each other's output. Decision-making teams are ones that have been authorized to make decisions about issues such as organizational goals, strategic policies or resource allocation. A relatively new concept is the global virtual team, which is built around technology. For global teams to run efficiently, they must take account of workers' different

FIGURE 3.5   Teams and functions

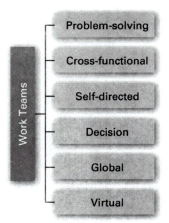

regions and time zones, particularly when members are asked to come together to discuss and/or make collective decisions. Thus global virtual teams rely heavily on technological media, including e-mail, instant messaging, Skype, Facetime, teleconferencing, videoconferencing and web casts, as well as social networking sites.

This brief overview of what constitutes groups and teams shows that the two are distinct even though the terms are often used interchangeably. The discussion will now move on to the development of teams.

Team development approaches

Team development is considered as a work in progress or, as defined by Gersick (1988: 9), 'the path a group takes over its life-span toward the accomplishment of its main tasks'. Two main research streams have contributed to the theories of team development. The first involves task and content-related functions, including task distribution, task demands, role clarity and individual inputs. The second explores the emotional and psychosocial aspects of team development, including group membership, integration and how individuals behave and relate to one another. With this in mind, six theories (many of which overlap) are introduced to highlight the psychological practices that underpin team development, because if team members grasp the nuances of group development and apply the theories, this will create better teams.

Functional approach

The first team development theory considered is Hare's (1976) functional approach to team development. This approach suggests that groups develop in four phases and in sequence (L-A-I-G). The model proposes four elements that are crucial to each phase. The first, 'latent' (L), is the need for members to accept and share common values and identify group goals. 'Adaption' (A) is the second element and refers to the necessary knowledge, skills and abilities (KSAs) and resources that enable the group to carry out their tasks. Element three is 'Integration' (I), which focuses on structural components that enable cooperation. The last element in the series is 'Goal-attainment' (G), which relates to how well group members can exercise control over their membership and have the know-how to coordinate the use of resources and roles in pursuit of their common goal.

The model claims that unless each element is working well in a given phase, groups will not be able to progress to the next one. Sometimes teams remain stuck in one particular phase or, in worse scenarios, never make it over the finishing line but break down before achieving their goal. While the model does provide a description of sub-phases and the impact these have on groups when moving from one phase to the next, the model is somewhat unclear about the timings of each phase and whether the time each takes depends on the leader's understanding of group dynamics and his/her ability to facilitate groups through their working stages. Furthermore, the theory fails to recognize that teams are naturally inclined to experience some degree of disruption. According to Tuckman and Jensen, this turbulence in fact moves teams forward. Which leads us to the next theory of team development: Tuckman and Jensen's Five-stage Model.

Five-stage Model

In 1965, Tuckman developed the Stages of Development Model in which four dimensions were identified: Forming, Storming, Norming and Performing. In 1977, in collaboration with Jensen, the researchers expanded the model, adding Adjourning to the sequence – making the Stages of Development a five-stage model (see Figure 3.6).

FIGURE 3.6 Stages of group development

SOURCE: Adapted from Tuckman and Jensen (1977).

The model proposes that groups undergo a sequence of four stages before reaching their full potential. Before any group can proceed to the next stage, members must see themselves as a cohesive unit. However, this process does not always run smoothly.

During the first stage, Forming, individuals tend to focus on task and people-related issues. This involves making sense of what needs to be done, what resources are available and how best the task can be achieved, as well as potentially exploring who could do what. At this stage, individuals also start to learn about each other. They test the waters to determine which behaviours are deemed acceptable and which are not – which is often shown in the reactions and cues of fellow group members. This explains why members during the 'getting to know phase' sometimes sense an air of artificiality. They may feel self-conscious and cautious, behave with extreme political correctness. However, this sense of awkwardness does not last for long, and the team changes as it moves into the Storming stage.

The Storming stage is the second phase of development and generally emerges when individuals begin their work. It is here that cracks begin to surface: personalities begin to affect the atmosphere, power struggles and control issues take centre-stage. As a result, differing opinions and task-related issues become apparent as members begin to detect a mismatch between what the job entails and what is expected. Sometimes resistance kicks in; members may show signs of stress in trying to establish new group processes or work practices, or battle against the demands put on them. Tuckman and Jensen's (1977) theory does not suggest any particular 'Storming' indicators, so in an attempt to fill this gap, we can identify the following examples to help teams see what is going on:

- sabotage;
- withholding information;
- unwillingness to share;
- social loafing.

The important point is that during the Storming stage members will experience unrest, at both personal and task level. Successful teams will be able to identify and acknowledge the turbulent stage they are in. It is this awareness, and the teams' willingness to resolve their issues, that will enable teams to move to the next stage: 'Norming'.

The Norming stage is a space for reflection and resolution. For the first time, needs can be expressed, questions are asked and members listen and feed back to one another. Attempts are made to iron out differences and members begin to realize the need for cohesiveness. Groups start to adopt a problem-solving mentality. Conflict is replaced by harmony and people learn to accept the idiosyncrasies of fellow members, even if personality clashes cannot be entirely resolved. At task level, uncertainties are brought to the table and clarity develops as to what needs to be done and what resources are required, and individual roles start to emerge.

Assuming members have settled their differences, the group can focus on Performing. In the Performing stage, members work inter-dependently and collectively to achieve their goal. They are clear on their given roles and individuals come to understand that the team functions better when they are united. Where necessary, problems are dealt with and support is given.

The fifth stage is Adjourning, which happens after groups have reached their goal. In some instances groups may disperse, leaving some individuals with feelings of melancholy – or of relief or euphoria. This stage is also known as 'Mourning', as members learn to cope with disengagement and potential feelings of loss. Typically, this may occur in project teams that have been formed on a temporary basis and disband when goals have been achieved.

It is still unclear whether the ideas of stages of group development can actually be applied to organizational life, since the theory was developed through the use of therapeutic groups (T-groups) in clinical settings and natural laboratory groups. Also, the model does not indicate how long each stage lasts or the mechanisms that initiate further development. Nor does it explain what impulses for change move the groups from one stage to another. Groups must expect bottlenecks, and the model does not account for issues going un-resolved or going underground (Poole, 1983). Nor does it envision that groups may go through the stages in varying order or even simultane-ously: for example, when groups storm and perform concurrently.

Sometimes groups may even regress to previous stages, suggesting the model may be more cyclical, depending on the nature of the task, the group dynamics and the role of the leader. Nonetheless, the model has been useful in our understanding of group development processes and it provided a platform for the development of further group development models, such as Lacoursiere's (1980) Life Cycle of Groups, which will be explored next.

Life Cycle of Groups

Lacoursiere's (1980) theory compares group cycles to the life stages of living organisms. The concept of a life cycle of groups provides interesting insights into group development. In his description, he argues that groups go through various stages and in doing so are subjected to a number of obstacles and stresses. The extent to which groups can manage these will determine whether they continue to exist. The model points out that within each stage there is a degree of overlap (in contrast to Tuckman and Jensen's model). Lacoursiere's model also consists of five stages: Orientation, Dissatisfaction, Resolution, Production and Termination.

Like Tuckman and Jensen's (1977) Forming stage, Orientation is the first stage described by Lacoursiere (1980), and consists of the initial coming together of groups. Members are curious about other group members and question the extent to which they will fit in. At the onset, they may display a sense of enthusiasm and willingness. At the same time, individuals feel anxious, as they are uncertain about what will be done and how, who will lead them, the skills and abilities required and how they will be able to contribute towards the bigger picture. Borja Manchado of the Four Seasons Hotel observes: 'It is about putting in front of the team a goal that is valid for all of them. I think it is more about making them feel they are part of something more important than themselves; that is the key.' This, notes Linda DeGrow, former general manager of Voith Industrial Services, 'requires that you put the team first, and yourself second'. This focus on others is also evidenced in the Royal Marines. According to Alan Litster: 'If you have a selfish gene in your body you will not make it through 18 months of basic training as an officer, or 32 weeks for a

Marine.' Alan goes on to say that 'a certain amount of self is trained out of you during the training process and you get used to subordinating your personal goals for those of the team'. These points are also emphasized by Bassin (1988), who argues that all team members must share a common vision that is greater than their own personal interests or individual agendas.

The second stage groups go through is Dissatisfaction, which is often the result of a mismatch between expectations and realities. For example, members may have hoped to gain something from their team experience, but find as time progresses that this is not happening. Consequently they start to feel frustrated. Lacoursiere (1980: 31) says that the 'length, intensity and actual placement of the Dissatisfaction stage within the experience' will depend on a number of factors, including the task's difficulty and other task-related issues, both of which will be discussed below.

Successful resolution will push groups into the Production phase and create higher morale and commitment to accomplishing the task. How long this takes will depend on the level and severity of issues, height of emotions, existing dynamics and, perhaps more importantly, the group's willingness to resolve matters. This stage also provides an opportunity for individuals to address expectations and to realign these with more realistic and tangible prospects. To achieve this, groups need to take time out in order to reassess task aims, revisit what needs to be done and, if necessary, redistribute roles and individual outputs.

In considering this, it is worth diverting the discussion for a moment to consider Steiner's (1972) task taxonomy, which distinguishes between types of tasks, task demands, task distribution and to what extent members' inputs work together. The taxonomy is divided into three categories: 'divisibility', 'focus' and 'interdependence'. The divisibility dimension determines whether the task is *unitary* or *divisible* (see Figure 3.7). Unlike unitary tasks, divisible tasks can be broken down into smaller sub-tasks and assigned to individual members. Steiner's second dimension focuses on *quantity* and *quality*. When outcome is determined by quantity, this means the goal is to maximize output – in contrast to optimization, where the goal is for teams to produce the best suitable outcome. Steiner's (1972) third dimension concerns interdependence – that is, the strategies, processes and task requirements imposed on the individual and group – is determined by the type of task: additive, compensatory, conjunctive, disjunctive or discretionary (see Figure 3.7). *Additive* tasks do not require interaction among group members; rather the group's product is the sum of all the members' outputs, which means individuals can work independently. *Compensatory* tasks do not require interaction between team members either, because here the group's product is the average of the individuals' inputs. *Disjunctive* tasks rely on interaction, but the ultimate decision or outcome is usually determined by the most competent of the group members. In contrast, *conjunctive* tasks rely on the input of all group members, so if any member does not complete his or her task the entire project will be stalled. Lastly, when relationships or working practices are not dictated by prescribed rules and when team members have the flexibility to choose their own processes, then tasks are referred to as *discretionary*. In order to reduce potential roadblocks, teams should evaluate the task requirements imposed on individuals early in the team-cycle process. This would best be done during the Orientation stage.

FIGURE 3.7   Three-dimension taxonomy

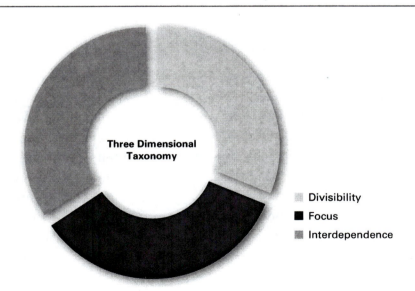

Three Dimensional Taxonomy

- Divisibility
- Focus
- Interdependence

SOURCE: Adapted from Steiner (1972).

Lacoursiere's Production stage is characterized by positivity and cohesiveness (as in Tuckman and Jensen's Performing stage). Once teams enter this state, members will feel more competent and show willingness to move forward. This is underpinned by explicit and implicit norms that have evolved throughout the process. As a result teams become more cohesive as well as accountable. Here, members realize that can only fulfil their purpose if they work together. Didier Souillat, managing director of Hakkasan, emphasizes this, explaining: 'We work as a team... You know that if you do not deliver your part, the team will suffer. So the team is cohesive and everyone does what is needed to make sure that nobody else suffers from their shortfall.' The term 'social loafing' describes the situation where members do not contribute to the group's work, and we will return to this in Chapter 4.

Once a group approaches the finishing line, members begin to reflect upon their own accomplishments, their group interactions and so on. How members respond depends on their overall experiences. Lacoursiere insists that most groups do reach the end point (Termination), though some – despite trying to do so – do not fully resolve their dissatisfaction. In extreme cases, this can lead to extinction or group disintegration.

Punctuated Equilibrium Model

The Punctuated Equilibrium Model (Gersick, 1988) claims that teams do not develop through a series of stages; instead, groups experience periods of stability or equilibrium. During the equilibrium period, group norms are devised and frameworks created that guide members' behaviour. At some point, however, the equilibrium 'seizes up'. This can occur when team members suddenly realize they are dangerously close to a deadline: a concept referred to as the mid-point crisis. This concept, or rather consciousness, moves teams into the second period, in which current working practices and processes are revisited in an attempt to improve group performance. New working methods are put in place and push the group towards completion.

Findings by Seers and Woodruff (1997) indicate that the Punctuated Equilibrium Model is particularly useful for groups working towards tight deadlines. While the model is useful in our understanding of change and how change develops over time, some have questioned whether the model fully explains processes of team development, arguing the 'mid-point crisis' may be the result of time constraints rather than a description of group development. And indeed, if mid-points create a transitional momentum, do they automatically guarantee progress? For example, a group may feel strongly that it is time to move ahead, yet be incapable of doing so for some reason. Conversely, even if progress is not visible on the surface, this does not imply there is no progress at all.

Team Organization Model

Tjosvold's (1991) Team Organization Model represents five team components that encourage team development and team effectiveness. These components are: Envision, Unite, Empower, Explore and Reflect (see Figure 3.8).

FIGURE 3.8   Team organization model

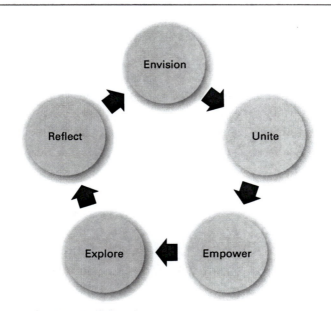

SOURCE: Adapted from Tjosvold (1991). With permission from the author.

The first component of the model, Envision, stresses the importance of creating a vision and of commitment towards it. Members can only envision if they understand what the vision entails. Santander UK's Human Resource Director Simon Lloyd clarifies this: 'Commonality of purpose is very important. [You can have] a genuine lack of alignment or lack of understanding if some people think the objective is A and other people think it is B. So if you are not aligned you will go off and do different things.' Tjosvold claims that only through collective participation will it be possible to employ a shared vision. What is important here, says Tjosvold, is for members to feel part of the shaping process. To aid this understanding, leaders should give team members space for questioning and opportunities to generate ideas. Useful forms of questioning could be about organizational objectives and how these can be met, as well as asking 'What is my role and the role of others around me?' While the list is not exhaustive, Tjosvold suggests several ways to ensure envisioning, including:

- Assess the business mission.
- Take risks and learn from mistakes.
- Dialogue.
- Include.
- Update.

Team leaders play an important role during the envisioning stage – so much so says Maike van der Hooghen of the Dutch MOD, that leadership is crucial 'to the success or failure of teams'. Louise Hill similarly affirms the importance of her leadership role in helping 'people to see the vision and to inspire them; then they will want to follow you and be excited about reaching that goal.' Qantas Chief Marketing Officer Lewis Pullen affirms this by saying: 'I think leadership is about having a very clear vision of where you are going and motivating a team of people to that vision.' Simon Lloyd expressed similar ideas: 'It's about a broader strategic vision; it is looking into the future, it is about taking people with you.' The message here according to Michael Aldous of the LSE, is that: 'You have to have good managers at different levels that provide clarity and leadership and bring people together.' The key point is that successful leaders will involve their members and, in return, get them on board. This is something Lewis Pullen knows all about; he remarks:

> I spent a lot of my life in sport and being a team captain and that is an interesting analogy to business. It's amazing what you'll do to follow the captain of the team, you put your body on the line, you'll do whatever it takes... [it's] no different in business. That's what leadership is about – someone who can galvanize a team.

These insights may be of particular interest to graduates who are considering leadership roles. The main discussion on leadership is reserved for Chapter 7, but in the meantime graduates might consider ways to develop best practices and work on the attributes that are said to promote good team leaders.

A united team shares a coherent vision and purpose, which incidentally forms the second component of Tjosvold's model. Henrietta Lovell of the Rare Tea Company says that 'making employees feel that they are part of the business can be a huge step forward, particularly in terms of commitment'. This step convinces members that the vision and commitment they share unites them. Thus for members to work as a team, they need to learn that they will only succeed by working together. A great leader, says Louise Hill, 'will know how to get the best from each individual, [be someone] who is able to see how each person contributes to the team and makes sure each member knows what everyone else brings'. Under this leadership, members will want to unite and move in the same direction. Yet, says Maike van der Hooghen, this does not just happen by itself. In her role as team leader she constantly emphasizes what has to be done: 'Every day I repeat what I expect from the team in briefings and discussions. It has to become second nature, a sort of culture, so that people feel motivated, connected and are proud of themselves and of their team and what they have accomplished.' To build team purpose, it is important to recognize all the members' ideas, needs and opinions and, Simon Lloyd points out, 'respect each other's competencies'. (We will return to this in Chapter 7.)

In a bid to bind individuals and the team closer to their goal, Guy Kendall (a former systems engineer at the National Theatre) says it is important to 'praise and encourage work both on an individual and team level whenever this is appropriate'. Since most reward systems are based on individual merit however, in a team setting this raises a problem in that individual rewards do little to promote collaboration. Stark, Shaw and Duffy (2007) therefore propose the development of team-based reward systems, which they claim will give teams a greater sense of accomplishment. Dyer, Dyer and Dyer (2007) also suggest that if organizations take the time to develop team-based reward systems, this could encourage team unity: the belief that without individual input the whole becomes less than the sum of its parts. Other research that shows why teamwork can be better than individuals working on their own suggests that it leads to:

- greater creativity and innovation (eg West, 2004);
- a reduction in absenteeism (eg Cotton, 1993);
- emotional support (eg Otten, Sassenberg and Kessler, 2009; Schutte *et al*, 2001);
- improvements in communication skills (eg Spiegel and Torres, 1994) and individual problem-solving (eg Albanese, 1994);
- social appeal (eg Mueller, Procter and Buchanan, 2000).

The practice of collaboration requires teams to communicate openly, to share information and knowledge so as to strengthen their unity in reaching their goal. In facilitating this process, members may need to adjust their interpersonal behaviours and/or working practices so as to align themselves more closely with each other. The following strategies proposed by Tjosvold (1991: 136–40) are useful for team leaders in helping to promote unity:

- Explore the team's vision.
- Make the task challenging.
- Praise the team as a whole for its success.
- Highlight everyone's abilities.
- Encourage team identity.
- Promote self-disclosure.

Once members feel united in their shared vision, the next step is the belief that they have the means to accomplish it, a belief that empowers team members to do just that. Team members have to believe they have the relevant skills, because this gives them the motivation and confidence to carry out their roles. Empowerment is also enhanced when members receive support from their organization at both the task and the social–emotional level. At the task level this means members have scope to make decisions and are supplied with everything they need to carry out their job. At the social–emotional level the focus is on recognition, where workers are acknowledged for their contribution and know they will receive emotional support if needed. If there is proper support and group norms develop, members will develop a sense of group membership. In facilitating empowerment, Tjosvold (1991: 152–54) suggests the following strategies:

- Relate the team's vision to that of the organization.
- Include skilled, relevant people.
- Hold individuals accountable.

A common theme in group development theories is that groups usually go through a period of turbulence. Conflicts are inevitable and surface as a result of interpersonal or job-related issues. A willing team will be keen to identify and explore these issues so that they can move forward. The million-dollar question is: how? The trick is to capture the mood swiftly and to allow members to air their views, even if conflicting. How teams ultimately manage their conflict will determine the group's course. This will be explored further in Chapter 4. Tjosvold (1991: 176–78) illustrates a variety of tactics to help facilitate the explorative process:

- Include diverse people.
- Ask questions.
- Work to resolve.

Which brings the Team Organization Model to its final stage, that of Reflection. The reflective stage gives individuals the opportunity to analyse their own contributions and the contributions made by the group. Effective teams learn from their mistakes, manage obstacles and understand their shortcomings. They are able to adapt and to analyse the changes required both in the present and for the future. Tjosvold (1991: 196–200) proposes a number of strategies that can assist teams in their reflective practices:

- Use questionnaires for general information and comparison.
- Interview for rich information.
- Put self in others' shoes.
- Strive for ongoing improvement.

Tjosvold's model is comprehensive and touches upon many aspects. In doing so, it is able to capture the highs and lows of team development processes and provide a wealth of tools for teams to work with. While there is some overlap with other theories, the Team Organization Model remains unique in its own right.

The Four Cs

The last model to promote high-performance teams is proposed by Dyer, Dyer and Dyer (2007), who identify four team elements, or 'four Cs'. These elements are context, composition, competency and change (see Figure 3.9).

Before any team is set up, Dyer, Dyer and Dyer (2007: 6) emphasize the need to establish early on whether the situation (whatever it may be) requires the establishment of teams and/or teamwork. In doing so, one must ask: 'Is effective teamwork critical to accomplishing the goals desired by the organization?', or can individuals achieve the required goals alone? A good example of this is illustrated by the academic Michael Aldous, who explains how the teamwork context varies in his role:

> I find it quite interesting; if you look at different components in an academic institution, teamwork is a really an odd issue. On the one hand, as a researcher, it really is just you in an archive or library reading, but [if you are] working with people in terms of co-writing then you have to understand how to manage and work with someone else.

FIGURE 3.9   The four Cs

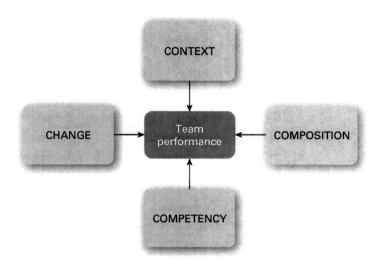

SOURCE: Dyer *et al*, 2007. With permission to reproduce from John Wiley & Sons.

On this topic, University Reader Samantha Faros affirms: 'Because each one of us is specialized in subject-specific areas, this means that most of my academic work I carry out alone. I think it would be counterproductive if some of my duties were to be spread out to other members of staff.' Context therefore is an important consideration, and despite the ongoing trend there are times, as the above examples indicate, where teamwork may not always be relevant. This is true for people as well as for fields of work.

Of particular interest is the commentary by Hugo Chapman of the British Museum:

> You have to be very careful in building that team from the beginning. This means that when putting teams together it is important to recognize that there are people you know who are good team people, and there are people who you know are not good team people. It is foolish to try and put non-team people in a team, because you know they are not good at it. Knowing who team players are and who are not is important.

Likewise, Louise Hill affirms that it is important to get 'the right fit for the job role – people who will support and enhance the one that exists – [and] remove anyone that doesn't want to go in the same direction or disrupts the existing team'. The message here is that not everyone fits in the Team-based Model, and for this reason Hugo Chapman notes it makes sense to

> build work projects around the skills of the people you work with. A feeling of common purpose is hugely important; if there is one member who is pulling in another direction, it is so destructive. So you have to be a good judge of character, to know that someone who likes to work by themselves is not a person to put in a big team, because they are not going to be happy.

This too I have come to accept: that not everyone is suited to work in teams. Of course this does not make teamwork in any way redundant. On the contrary, teams play a pivotal part in organizational success, as notary public Riccardo Genghini, of Studio Notarile, Genghini and Associati, affirms: 'Teams are a necessity for succeeding today.' Or as hospitality industry leader Borja Manchado, declares: 'Hotels cannot work without a team,' and Professor Guy Samama, formerly of University Hospital Caen, affirms: 'Any surgeon must have a team.'

Thus, to the earlier context-related question posed by Dyer, Dyer and Dyer (2007) of whether groups perform better than individuals, Steiner (1972) replies firmly that they do, but equally recognizes groups' shortcomings. For example, groups outperform individuals (even the best individual) during additive tasks, and do better than most individuals during compensatory tasks; when it comes to disjunctive tasks however, groups' performance will be no better than that of the best individuals and may be worse, while with conjunctive tasks, groups' performance is equal to the worst individual's performance (Hogg and Vaughan, 2010). Lastly, Steiner explains that the reason why groups do not always reach their full potential is due to 'process losses'. A loss, says Steiner, may be caused by two factors: who is in the group and how members fit together. It is this 'fitting together' (composition), that forms the setting for Dyer, Dyer and Dyer's second element of the Four C Model.

Key to successful teams, they say, is to create the right balance of people, where each individual brings unique elements to the table. To build a team with the right skill sets early in the process, you must find members equipped with the necessary knowledge, skills and abilities (KSAs) and experience. The ultimate challenge, says Riccardo Genghini, is 'finding people that are complementary in their skills and compatible in character'.

This means, says Michael Aldous, that effective leaders will need to have the insight to 'recognize different skill sets and different personalities and how then they can build those together to make teams work'. Part of this process, Guy Kendall explains, is 'being versatile and understanding that people are not all the same. Acknowledging that strengths and weaknesses are present in everybody and managing these within the team.'

Looking at team leadership from a different angle, Simon Lloyd depicts the role of leaders in the context of team sport:

> I love sport and I think sport is a great analogy. If you look at a football team, you cannot have 11 goalkeepers and hope to succeed. You need a blend of skills, and that works in a business context as well. Being able to recognize the right skill sets in the team and then blending those team players together and getting them working effectively together – that is a key role of a manager.

Another interviewee to use this analogy was Jon Hall, sports and performance specialist managing director of PGIR Limited and former Bath rugby player, who explains that the reasons for Bath's success were both talented players and their coach: 'We had a good team, good skills, good players, a good backbone of leaders and we had somebody at the top that knew how to tweak and apply the right amount of influence to each player. He understood the players very well.'

So what are the team skill sets (KSAs) or ingredients that employers are keen to observe among team members? Of the 32 industry leaders interviewed – and in close alignment with team theorists (eg Dyer, Dyer and Dyer, 2007; Tjosvold, 1991; Tuckman and Jensen, 1977) – most agreed on similar sets (see Table 3.1).

For Alan Litster, trust is one team characteristic the Royal Marines cannot do without: 'Ultimately what we ask them to do is at such extreme ends of anybody's operating model that they have to trust each other completely and there is a certain amount of subordinating

TABLE 3.1   Industry leaders' preferred team attributes (N = 32)

Collaboration	Empathy
Competency	Resourceful
Support	Willing
Communication	Openness
Interpersonal	Accountable
Trust	Motivation
Flexibility	Reliable
Shares	Knowledge-sharing
Decision-making	Listening
Innovative	Engaging

self in terms of overall organizational aim.' In building trust explains Linda DeGrow, the key ingredient is: 'To share values and dreams and stay focused on reaching collective goals, not individual goals.' Joris Luyendijk, former Middle East Correspondent of NRC Handelsblad, believes: 'People need to be able to rely on management to stick with the parameters it has set out with trust and decisiveness.' Linda DeGrow, adds that: 'Fostering an environment of openness and candour helps to build trust among team members, which ultimately strengthens the team spirit and camaraderie.'

Developing this theme, Henrietta Lovell observed: 'People may have the right skills and relevant experience, but what really matters, is how they fit together and how the team functions as a unit.' Skills can often be learnt, but attitudes are much harder acquired. In the same vein, Novotel general manager Guy Lootens, stated: 'Attitude for me is the most important thing – I do not have a problem if a waiter cannot handle a bottle of champagne; what I do have a problem with is when the waiter does not say "hello" to a guest.' He sees such things as essential in the hospitality industry; to have an effective team, he believes, one needs a good working relationship.

The one theme that is recurs consistently throughout the interviews is the importance of attitude. There is a general consensus that employers are drawn to those with the right attitude and mindset over and above anything else (see Chapter 2).

Returning to Dyer's point about team composition and balance, Parker (2003) claims that the relationship between group size and group effectiveness is also influenced by the amount of resources provided and the KSAs possessed by individuals. To begin with, size does matter according to Steiner (1972), who concluded that as group size increases, productivity slows down because of the shared/ diffused responsibility for the overall outcome, which gives rise to 'social loafing' (see Chapter 4). Maximilien Ringelmann (1913) tested this hypothesis on a group of agricultural students in a tug-of-war, measuring how hard they pulled on the rope. He found that individuals' efforts decreased as the group increased in size. This is termed the Ringelmann effect. Needless, to say, there are different views about what the ideal group size is, with estimates ranging from four to six (Ringelmann, 1913; Parker, 2003), two to three (James, 1951) or 3 to 12 (Campion, Medsker and Higgs, 1993).

The third aspect of team efficiency proposed by Dyer, Dyer and Dyer (2007) is competency. Competencies in this context are not specifically related to individuals' KSAs; rather, they are embedded and become attributes of the whole group. Each team will have a set of competencies that is unique to itself. Which competencies these are will depend on the context and the balance of team members, though two are particularly pertinent: communication and conflict resolution. As mentioned earlier, conflict will be addressed in Chapter 4.

The researchers claim that a vital part of team success is communication: the exchange of and sharing of information. KLM flight despatcher (and trained pilot) Robert de Vos explains that in his work:

> It's very important because you have to relay information to your
> team, but in your daily job too you have to communicate with
> air traffic control. We have a clearly defined policy for how we

communicate and everybody has to stick to it to make sure there are no miscommunications, because it is really easy for misunderstandings to happen in stressful situations. Especially with flying, where clearances are given or when commands are given, it's really important to be clear and concise and [ensure] everybody knows what is meant, otherwise things can get out of control really fast.

Similarly, Linda DeGrow affirms: 'Developing a high-performance team begins with regular, clear and effective communication – vertically and horizontally. The team needs to know why they exist, what the mission is, what the goals are.' In promoting effective practices, organizational cultures (see Chapter 5) must be founded upon openness and transparency. This subject came up in an interview with Peter Stevenhagen, Scientific Director of the Mathematical Institute of Leiden University:

Managers tend to think of transparency as having some sort of a clear-cut procedure that you simply follow to make decisions. For me the ultimate aim, whenever there is broad consensus about it, is more important than any particular procedure, so from that point of view I'm completely non-transparent, in the sense that we do not follow predefined procedures.

Peter's stance is insightful – and different from the usual analyses of what you call transparent. Peter insists that openness and good judgement on the leader's part are the psychological mechanisms that make for good communication.

The capacity for change is the final element listed by Dyer, Dyer and Dyer (2007: 75). It not only gives high-performing teams 'the understanding of what is impeding their performance but [enables them] to take corrective action to achieve their goals'. They claim that high-performing teams monitor ongoing working practices and have the flexibility and adaptability to respond to change. Changes in teamworking practices may be triggered by either internal influences (eg restructuring, monitoring performance) or external ones (eg globalization, historical occurrences, competitors). They may also occur because of technological changes, as this comment by Microsoft's Dave Coplin illustrates: 'In the old days we all had to go to the office because that's where all the computers and machinery were, but we live in a really different world now; we don't need to be like that.'

Changes are made so that teams can continue to move forward. Change is threatening, yet the biggest challenge is in how we choose to work with each other – now and in the future. For example, Henrietta Lovell says, 'Without kindness it is pretty hard to work in a team' and Linda DeGrow asserts: 'Trust, respect, accountability and commitment go a long way in forming a solid foundation for a successful team.' Dyer, Dyer and Dyer (2007) provide a useful framework of how to help teams improve their working practices, proposing that when all four main elements are in place there is one thing that distinguishes effective teams from ineffective ones: real change comes from within. In pursuing this, Louise Hill suggests, there must above all be an aspiration 'to make a positive difference or believe that you can make a positive difference to the world. What kind of world you want to live in and how you can contribute to creating that world, even if it's only in a small way.'

Conclusion

This overview of the main team theories suggests that most analysts believe that teams usually go through a series of stages before reaching their full potential. It also seems that teams function best when tasks require multiple skill sets from a wide range of individuals. Teams succeed when task-related functions are clearly set out and the necessary resources are supplied. Successful teams pay attention to the emotional and psychosocial needs of their members and, in particular, recognize the importance of team members' contributions. Moreover, effective teams are good at identifying bottlenecks. In doing so, they step back, reflect and make adjustments accordingly.

Members who share the right skill sets and attributes contribute to team success. The key point is that pooling talent in a joint effort will – if led effectively – create group synergy. Synergy in turn builds cohesiveness. Also of great significance are the roles of team leaders, who are tasked not only with communicating the vision but with motivating a team of people to commit to it. The general consensus is that teamwork is inherent to organizational life. Sometimes however, teams can fall victim to the psychological intricacies of teamworking life. The next chapter will move on to discuss these intricacies and, ultimately, how potential barriers can be converted into best practice. Following up on that, Chapter 5 will discuss the significance of organizational culture and how this determines the pathway and practices to which team-based organizations commit.

Barriers and intricacies

Following the discussion of the major team development theories in Chapter 3, this chapter focuses on the psychological dynamics that hinder teamwork. Why do some teams fail? What can we do to help teams that are not functioning effectively? To answer these questions, insights will be provided from industry leaders and from social psychological theories of groupthink, conformity and social loafing. Other obstacles known to hamper teamwork, such as inappropriate roles and conflict, will also be discussed. The chapter provides insights on how to recognize barriers to teamwork, and will suggest that with the right intervention tools, even the most problematic teams can function.

Groupthink

In Chapter 3 it was noted that effective teams need a certain level of cohesiveness. This does not always translate into group effectiveness, however. In fact, too much cohesiveness comes at a price – the question being, what price? According to Microsoft's Chief Envisioning Officer Dave Coplin, one cost is that people hesitate to deviate from group norms:

> If you spend all of your time with your colleagues, you end up with this variant of groupthink. As we work for the same company, we are very similar in the same sort of generic scale: we are the same type of people, we work in the same type of industry, we have the same type of customers who have the same type of problems; so you end up with this narrow view of the world.

This phenomenon, explains Janis (1982: 9), is the result of groupthink – the first potential barrier in a series of team hindrances, defined as 'a mode of thinking that people engage in when they are deeply involved in a cohesive in-group, when the members' striving for unanimity overrides their motivation to realistically appraise alternatives courses of action'.

Groupthink can be divided into three elements: overestimation, closed-mindedness and unanimity. Each category manifests a variety of symptoms (see Table 4.1) known to cause defective decision-making (Janis, 1972).

TABLE 4.1   Groupthink constructs

Category	Symptom description
Overestimation	Disproportionate optimism Ignoring moral considerations
Closed-mindedness	Collective rationalization Excessive stereotyping
Uniformity	Pressure to conform Self-censorship

SOURCE: Adapted from Janis (1977).

The first category, overestimation, can give rise to an illusion that the group is invulnerable. This invulnerability leads to 'disproportionate optimism' and encourages risk-taking behaviours. Effectively, group members lose sight of reality by ignoring ethical considerations or moral implications in the lead-up to decision-making. Such overestimation leads to errors of judgement.

The second category is closed-mindedness. When groups fall victim to stereotypical mind-sets, 'collective rationalization' sets in. This means that members of the group will go to great lengths, even ostracizing those who do not fit in, to protect the group from any threat that could destabilize it (Gruter and Masters, 1986). Because they resist outside influences, group members are less likely to be exposed to new points of view. This serves to maintain the status quo. Guy Kendall, a former systems engineer at the National Theatre, confirms it is equally important to

> keep an open mind to different working practices or differing means
> to achieve a goal. I have had experience of junior team members
> who have seen a problem from a different view and have suggested
> viable alternatives – keeping an open mind allows these possibilities.
> Sometimes this would enable a change of direction, sometimes not.
> The opposite would be tending toward arrogance and a closed mind-set.

When teams fail to examine information or explore alternative solutions, these so-called 'minimally acceptable solutions' undermine the group's ability to make sound decisions.

The third category associated with groupthink is uniformity. Teams characterized by uniformity may not allow members to deviate from their group norms. Those who hold different views or make a stand against the group become labelled as disloyal. According to Festinger, Schachter and Back (1950), consensus-seeking behaviour is more prevalent in groups where members feel pressured or when there is an uneven distribution of power. In such circumstances, group members adhere to the majority view, often from fear of retaliation or 'scape-goating'. When members choose to remain compliant, or hide their dissenting views, Janis (1982) describes this as 'self-censorship'. This means that members are willing to sacrifice their individual opinions, often at the expense of dissonance, in a bid to preserve existing agreements and group harmony.

Interestingly, cultural factors have been found to affect conformity (Ng and Van Dyne, 2001). It appears to be more prevalent in collectivist societies (such as Colombia, Costa Rica, Ecuador, Guatemala, Panama, El Salvador, Indonesia, Pakistan, Portugal, Taiwan) than in individualistic nations (like the United States or Canada). In some East Asian regions (eg Korea and China) conformity is even considered a positive trait (Kim and Markus, 1999). Hofstede's (1980) explanation for this is anchored in the way people in some societies have been socially conditioned with an emphasis on 'we' rather than on 'I' (see also Adler, 1991). In collectivist societies people learn about integration at a young age (Smith *et al*, 1994). Cultural frames of references and social orientations determine their view that they should look out for each other. The result is that in collective cultures individuals will be more likely to conform, and that cultural differences in conformity may be more acceptable in different cultural contexts. This collectivist thinking also explains why social loafing, which will be discussed later, is less prevalent in collectivist societies because people are more sensitive to how others perceive them.

Conformity is also determined by the relationship between group members. In helping to understand how groups use social influence, Turner (1996: 3) refers to the concept of the social norm: that is, 'a generally accepted way of thinking, feeling or behaving that is endorsed and expected because it is perceived as the right and proper thing to do'. Two sets of influencing styles are known to direct conformity: *informational* social influence and *normative* social influence. The former describes the process in which people collectively gather and rely on each other's information. Individuals do this to feel reassured about their sense of reality; hence, they turn to others as a frame of reference for information-seeking behaviours (see Figure 4.1). This need for information is central to the concept of social comparison theory (Festinger, 1954), which argues that people are keen to evaluate their own ideas and attitudes in relation to others.

FIGURE 4.1   The relationship between informational influence and conformity

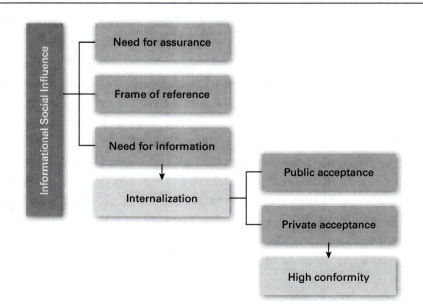

Informational social influence is further underpinned by internalization (see Figure 4.1); that is, 'when a change in behaviour or opinion is in alignment with a public belief or opinion' (Kelman, 1958). In this case conformity takes its strongest form – 'true conformity' (Mann, 1969) – because the individual's norms have altered because he or she has accepted the beliefs and values supporting the collective norm.

The second factor that directs conformity is normative social influence (see Figure 4.2). Conformity here is less intense because the individual involved is not privately convinced of the majority's position. In contrast to informational social influence, people accept others' feelings and expectations (ie public acceptance) in response to group pressure, often led by those in positions of authority who have the power to reject, accept, reward, or punish. Individuals thus comply and align themselves to the group in order to fit in and to safeguard their position (Asch, 1952).

Studies by Sherif (1936) and Asch (1952) observe that conformity 'reflects a rational process in which people construct a norm from other people's behaviour in order to determine correct and appropriate

FIGURE 4.2　The relationship between normative influence and conformity

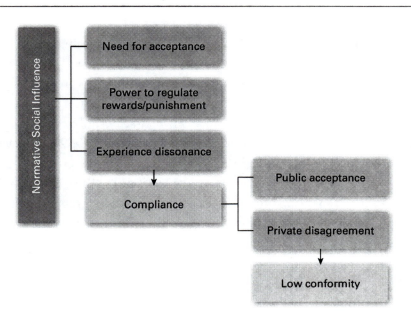

behaviour for themselves' (Hogg and Vaughan, 2010: 127). Links to self-esteem and validation explain why some people succumb to social pressure more readily than others, and this has generated much interest among humanistic psychologists. Both Maslow (1954) and Rogers (1961) discuss this in relation to the humanistic concept of the self: that is, the beliefs one has about oneself. According to Rogers, three sets of perceptions are inherent to the self-concept: self-worth, self-image and the ideal self. These stem from our need for positive regard (love, affection, nurturance, intimacy) and positive self-regard (self-worth, self-esteem, positive self-image). This innate yearning is so fundamental that it intrinsically determines how worthy we feel. Self-worth is cultivated during the early stages of life by those closest to us (eg parents, carers, peers, educators, society). This can be manifest in two ways: first, self-worth (self-esteem) will be at its lowest when positive regard is based on conditions of worth, and second, will be strongest when positive regard is given to us unconditionally. The problem starts when individuals have a sense of worth that is not matched in society or their immediate surroundings. This triggers an incongruity. Rogers maintains that this incongruity blurs the boundaries between our real self and the ideal self. As a result, people start to measure their degree of self-worth through the validation of others. Thus those who experience low self-worth are more susceptible to conforming, because they are seeking approval.

Since compliance does not create an internal or permanent shift in opinion (see Fgure 4.2), in the long-term individuals will struggle. At some point there will be dissonance between their private beliefs and those they conform to (ie public acceptance). This ties in closely with the concepts of private acceptance (ie real-self), public acceptance (ie ideal self) and normative social influence (Asch, 1952), that were discussed earlier. This is in stark contrast to the critical social psychologies described by social constructionists (Burr, 1995), who believe it is redundant to draw upon others for references, as each person constructs their own version of reality and view of the world. Social constructionists thus suggest there is no absolute truth or objective fact about human nature, people or society. Rather, the social constructionist view is founded upon historical and cultural relativism (eg values, beliefs) of all forms of knowledge (eg past experiences).

Social loafing

Social loafing is the second potential barrier to effective group work, and is described by Karau and Williams (1993: 681) as 'the reduction in individual effort when individuals work on a collective task compared to when they work on an individual task'. This is also termed the 'free-rider effect'. In Chapter 3, associations were made between social loafing, tasking and individual input. Similarly, this chapter affirms the task aspect, following Karau and Williams (1993) who concluded in a meta-analysis of 78 studies that team members are likely to produce less effort when a task has no clear purpose or does not add value to the individual. In this instance, individuals are more than happy to drain the resources made available to them, but unwilling to contribute as part of the whole. A second explanation for social loafing suggests that the mere presence of other group members permits loafers to go undetected. This in particular occurs when group are large or when performance is not well monitored, and is sometimes termed 'output equity' (Jackson and Harkins, 1985). Under these conditions loafing becomes almost inevitable.

With these descriptions in mind, the chapter will now present a new perspective on social loafing, in an effort to understand its underlying causes and how to manage them. From my own experience, the following loafing behaviours have been observed:

- disengagement;
- defensiveness;
- missing deadlines;
- non-communication;
- lack of interest;
- aloofness;
- passive aggressiveness.

This suggests that in organizational settings some individuals can disengage from difficult situations. The question is why? Could the decision to defect be the result of task-related anxiety? Or could individuals withdraw as a result of socio-emotional stress? For example, at task level, one reason may be that individuals feel uncertain about tasks or individual roles, which leads to feelings of anxiety or incompetence. This could demotivate and push individuals to withdraw, possibly from fear of ridicule. Similarly, at the socio-emotional level it may be because individuals feel devalued or redundant in comparison to other group members. Other explanations for disengagement can be sought in the sphere of personality. For example, differences in personality traits can lead to clashes, which in turn may affect how individual team members behave to one another.

While loafing is unpleasant, the real issue is what to do about it. The best way to tackle it is early in the process by readdressing both socio-emotional and task-related aspects. First off, team leaders and their members would be wise to identify and consider prospective behaviours such as those outlined above. The ultimate aim is to get the person back on board and fully engaged. Chief Marketing Officer Lewis Pullen believes: 'a lot of that is about engaging with people right in the beginning in terms of the pathway to that vision, making them feel they are party to it.' He goes on to say: 'If people are led inspirationally then people will buy in and be willing to contribute.' One way to get people on board is to remind individuals of the pivotal role they play and of their unique abilities. As Linda DeGrow puts it: 'Team members need to know why they and all other members are on the team – what innate and technical skills they bring to it.' This is particularly helpful when individuals feel undervalued. Another way to regulate social loafing says Maike van der Hooghen, Branch Head at the Dutch MOD, is to 'stress the importance of a professional work attitude, discipline, responsibility, cooperation and communication' from the onset of any teamwork activity. This means, adds Linda DeGrow, 'holding each other accountable for performance and meeting obligations'.

When handling loafing behaviours it is therefore important to be mindful of how individuals feel. This would require a change in mind-set, one that does not point the finger too quickly at someone or think the worst of people and does not lead to ostracism to regulate behaviours (see for example Williams, Cheung and Choi, 2000). As Royal Marine Alan Litster explains: 'Our teams can be very self-selecting – we are talking groups of young men, so lots of testosterone.

If someone is not pulling their weight or if somebody is not conforming to the group dynamic then that person could be ostracized by the team.' While this may be optimal for Royal Marine life, Robinson, O'Reilly and Wang (2013) believe social exclusion does more harm than good. At both the individual and the organizational level, they believe it can harm emotional and psychological well-being as well as productivity (Wesselmann *et al*, 2012).

Some readers may think loafing behaviour is not their problem. The truth is that it is everyone's problem, and to think otherwise is the chief reason why so many working environments lack genuine camaraderie (or, as Henrietta Lovell of the Rare Tea Company puts it, 'when one person either does not care or does not understand the needs of other team members'). By recognizing and incorporating the above practices it is possible to keep loafing in check, even though CEO of Cognisess Chris Butt rightly observes that 'breaking old patterns can be challenging: reversing poor habits is incredibly difficult and unlearning them is tough.' Nonetheless industry leader Lewis Pullen believes it can be done, 'as long as you help them understand the vision and allow them to participate.'

Conflict resolution

In Chapter 3, it was pointed out that a certain degree of heterogeneity among team members is valuable, as it provides differing perspectives and greater scope for new ideas. The flipside of this is that too much heterogeneity creates problems, even grounds for conflict and disagreement, because individuals find it difficult to share common ground. Conflict can have other causes, as Human Resource Director of L'Oréal, Isabelle Minneci explains: 'Turmoil can be the result of a lack of direction/clear strategy, communication/transparent information-sharing, lack of efficiency and decision-making; this can lead to irritation.' Similarly, when team members do not fully grasp the wider extent or context of each other's roles, confusion can arise about the expectations and obligations of each individual team member. As Ward Edmonds, manager of TrateMedia, affirms, if 'goals and targets are not clearly delineated, defined or understood or, conversely, unrealistic goals/targets have been set, this can create tensions.' Or, when the team members are unclear about the task or team role they play, tasks might go unattended. This too can cause conflict, particularly when members rely heavily on one another (as outlined in Steiner's task taxonomy discussed in Chapter 3). Thus, conflict arises for various reasons.

In managing conflict, Dyer, Dyer and Dyer (2007) stipulate that what distinguishes effective from non-effective teams is recognizing the type of conflict and that conflict is sometimes inevitable (as, for example, at Tuckman and Jensen's Storming stage – see Chapter 3). Indeed, not all conflict is negative: properly dealt with it can improve group dynamics or even strengthen relationships (Tjosvold, 1991). Four types of conflict have been identified: in brief, intrapersonal conflict, which involves the individual alone; interpersonal conflict between two or more people who are in opposition to one another; inter-group conflict with members of different teams; and inter-organizational conflict between companies that share similar markets and therefore are in competition with one another.

In managing conflict it is important to understand the stress signals that accompany conflict. Potential signals can range from aggressive to passive aggressive behaviours, lethargy indecisiveness, extreme competitiveness and withdrawnness (Lewicki *et al*, 2001). As Alan Litster points out: 'You can tell where a team is not working because their performance, or lack of it, is pretty stark.'

An additional conflict resolution practice that effective teams display is knowing how to address and resolve team issues early on: if they do not, unresolved conflict can lead to patchy relations and a downward spiral in performance. For this reason, affirms Riccardo Genghini of Studio Notarile Genghini and Associati, sooner rather than later, 'petty personal issues at work must be effectively eradicated, because they have result in levelling performance down to the lowest common denominator'. When dealing with interpersonal conflict, for example, the knack is to redirect the focus away from the personal and instead to draw attention back to the bigger picture, the goal, the task itself. One method of dealing with the latter is to distinguish between the people involved and the actual problem. This is useful because 'conflict lies not in objective reality, but in people's heads' (Fisher and

Ury, 1991: 22), a view also shared by social constructionists. Conflict resolution requires those in conflict to re-evaluate their own perceptions and those of others, taxing as this may be: 'putting ourselves in someone else's shoes can reduce pre-conceived judgements, and allows the parties to understand each other's convictions. This ability to recognize team needs involves a degree of emotional intelligence' (Fisher and Ury, 1991) Linda DeGrow manages this through training, explaining: 'all of the managers on my team were trained in "Crucial Conversations", so they had skills and tools to deal effectively with conflict. Sharing knowledge and doing cross-training where appropriate helped to build my team's efficiency.'

This means allowing members to communicate what is on their minds. Remember, though, that messages can sometimes be misinterpreted because of a misalignment between the ways that 'what' and 'how' messages are communicated, as discussed in Chapter 1. Birdwhistell (1971) and Mehrabian (2007) claim it is not the words per se that cause confusion or misunderstanding, nor the sequence in which they are compiled; instead, the authors claim it is the circumstances in which they are communicated and what the body language projects (see Table 4.2), especially when negative emotions are involved.

The case for non-verbal communication was made in Darwin's *The Expression of the Emotions in Man and Animals* (1872) and has been developed through research across various disciplines, including cultural anthropology (eg La Barre, 1947), biology, anthropology (eg Birdwhistell, 1971), psychology and psychiatry (eg Ruesch, 1966). Overall, researchers broadly agree on a 'corpus of non-verbal cues', with Brannigan and Humphries (1972: 406) claiming 'over 80 [nonverbal] elements arising from the face and head and a further 55 produced by the body and limbs', and Grant (1969) claiming 116 elements. Non-verbal signals convey people's emotional states through expressions, tone of voice and posture (Davitz, 1964). If we can identify conflict-related signals alongside non-verbal communication cues, this could help defuse potential conflict situations.

TABLE 4.2   Non-verbal communication stress indicators

Gestures of negative NVC behaviours	Possible meaning
Too little eye contact, closed posture, limited verbal communication, lack of warmth	Lack of empathy Suspicion Withholding information
Frowning, constricted pupils, tense posture, pursed lips, furrowed brow, flared nostrils, rigid body, lack of movement, nervousness	Unhappiness/ dissatisfaction
Constant interruption, evidence of poor listening	Lack of agreement
Shaking head, frowning, tense crossing of arms, hiding mouth, crossing legs away from speaker	Disagreement, disapproval
Erratic breathing, yawning, lack of eye contact, arms/legs crossed, leaning away	Lack of receptiveness
Looking away, hunched shoulders, face placid, vacant eyes, sighing, finger drumming	Lack of interest/ distraction
Arching fingers to a peak, patting others on the back, invading others' space, initiating arching and terminating transactions	Feeling of superior status
Accentuated breathing, intense stance, aggressive eye contact, face taut, clenched fists, finger stabbing	Anger or irritation
One eyebrow, crooked smile, tilted head	Disbelief
Rubbing end of nose, breaking eye contact erratically, moving eyes upwards to (their) right when responding, nervous hand/leg movements, incongruity between words and body movement	Potential lack of honesty

SOURCE: John Walkley Associates © NLP/Assessment.

Conclusion

The catchphrase 'Together everyone achieves more' encapsulates one reason why organizations are keen to implement teams. It is widely thought that pulling together unique talents will equate to team 'synergy' (Allen and Hecht, 2001). The chapter has outlined the differing barriers to effective teamwork, with a focus on groupthink, uniformity and conformity. Teams need a well-balanced mixture of people, roles and viewpoints as well as a degree of homogeneity. Other potential barriers include social loafing and how this ultimately affects all members of an organization. High-performing teams thus need to equip themselves with conflict resolution skills to facilitate personal and/or task-related matters. Key to effective teams is the role of leadership (see Chapter 6) and the culture in which team-based organizations can thrive. Chapter 5 will explore the concept of organizational culture, as this will further influence the success or failure of teams.

Organizational culture

05

J ust as there are cultural differences between nations, there are cultural differences between organizations; the culture of an organization affects the behaviour of each individual in it and defines the environment in which work takes place. This chapter describes the importance of organizational culture and provides an overview of research into the roots from which it grows. The chapter will begin by defining organizational culture and the different elements that form it. The importance of job control and decision-making latitude will also be considered, with reference to Karasek's (1979) Job Demand Control (JDC) Model. In addition, there will be a brief discussion of the impact of technology in the workplace and how it affects everyday life. The chapter concludes that thriving organizations foster cultures that are supportive and empowering, and are open and receptive towards change.

What is culture?

Culture is best defined as:

> a pattern of basic assumptions, invented, discovered, or developed by a given group, as it learns to cope with its problems of external adaptation and internal integration, that has worked well enough to be considered valid and, therefore is to be taught to new members as the correct way to perceive, think, and feel in relation to those problems (Schein, 1990: 111).

An organization that values its culture will prescribe shared beliefs, values and rules for behaviour. This is said to give members of an organization a sense of identity as it sets a standard for how they should talk, behave and act to others. Not only does it set this standard for members inside the organization, but for those outside as well; for example, a human resource department that shows courtesy throughout its selection practices would project an ethos of care. In the long term, organizations cannot operate (successfully) without a clearly defined culture.

Building culture

How then is organizational culture built? The first way to develop it is through the influence of its group members (ie collectively), and the second is through the actions of its leaders (top-down). Beginning with the first, one suggestion is that culture is built through the practice of joint learning (Schein, 2010). This means that members collectively arrive at behavioural patterns through a process of trial and error (Drennan, 1992). In doing so, members observe each other's actions and communicate what they like or dislike through forums and meetings (Sagiv and Schwartz, 2007). If certain practices are a frowned upon by members, new ones are sought and norms slowly begin to take shape. This approach requires the collaboration and commitment of all members (where possible) across the organization.

The second approach to building a culture places the onus on its leaders. While leaders are not solely responsible for culture, Nicholson (1984) argues they are best suited to direct a unified culture around core ethical values, the organization's vision or mission statement. Qantas Chief Marketing Officer Lewis Pullen, however, argues that in building culture it is important to include all members of the organization. This means driving culture and pursuing value systems from the bottom up. He says:

> I spend a lot of time understanding how staff feel about the brand –
> whether they believe in it and subscribe to its values. For example when

we were building a new strategy for repositioning the Qantas brand, we went out and did a whole lot of workshops with all the frontline people – check-in staff, baggage handlers, engineers. We started top-down, but then went bottom up, pressure testing the brand strategy with the frontline to see if it made sense. We ended up tweaking it because some of those values were more important to certain groups than others, but generally they said yes that makes sense; they accepted the fundamental core of what we came up with, with four values for the organization: care, forward thinking, wisdom based on experience and 'contemporary Australia'.

What this implies is that culture building takes time and effort, and demands that those who drive it have a degree of openness. Also, in driving any culture forward it is important to be mindful of ethical considerations. It is this sense of 'correctness' that ultimately determines the pathways organizations decide to take – rightly or wrongly – as explained by Evanita ten Napel of Mitsubishi UFJ Securities, who provides a snapshot of how ethical considerations can manifest themselves: 'In my previous job it was all about how much money I brought in. All the important elements that make a good employee were considered less important than the amount of money you made for the bank.' This in sharp contrast to her current workplace:

> I would say at Mitsubishi it is absolutely not like that, we are less focused on the money than other banks might be because we are building up the company; money is still important, but the way this bank looks after its employees is completely different – they really try to make it a happy environment.

The two opposite approaches to organizational culture highlighted by Evanita's experiences mirror the task-orientated and person-orientated approaches to work.

The question of ethics concerns what we should do and how we should act as human beings, and the roles we choose to play in society or as part of a group. Since culture and ethics are so closely entwined, it is difficult to know whether it is the culture per se that determines ethics, or if the individuals' own ethical practices define (or fail to define) the behaviour of an organization's members (Ewin, 1991).

Here our emphasis is on ethical concerns: questions about what type of organization it will be, what value systems it will adopt, its relations to employees or clients, shareholders and stakeholders. Another company that is clear about its direction is described by resort manager Borja Manchado who proudly says:

> At the Four Seasons we have one golden rule: 'You treat others the way you want to be treated.' In every hotel or country we go to, we start from that single concept and we build the culture around it, and every decision we take that affects people has to be based on that golden rule. So yes, that is our motto.

At the Mill, clearly defined value systems are also observed, as co-founder and Chief Creative Director Pat Joseph describes:

> Integrity is part of the DNA of the Mill – it has been from day one. If you do not treat people well and you don't respect them, they will not respect you. Once you establish your business as an inclusive, caring business, that ethos will perpetuate itself. My legacy is to make sure that when I leave the business, it has fundamental principles that will live on.

Irrespective of how it is developed (collectively, top-down or both), culture is reinforced by a unique set of symbols, artefacts, rituals, unwritten rules, values, shared meanings and habits specific to each organization, some of which are visible while others work 'beneath the surface' (see Figure 5.1).

FIGURE 5.1 The Attribution Model

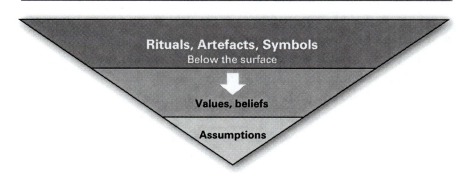

Rituals, Artefacts, Symbols
Below the surface

Values, beliefs

Assumptions

Symbols, artefacts and rituals are visible and represent the cultural manifestations of organizational life. Symbols, in the form of stories, myths, ritualized events and artefacts, help shape the way members think about their organization. Artefacts too convey meanings; here we think of aspects such as office space and layout, what clothes people wear, atmosphere and administrative elements such as mission statements. Ritual events also reinforce organizational culture. These may be ceremonies that mark important events such as promotions, milestones, successes or retirements, and parties before festive holidays.

Values and assumptions, on the other hand, are non-visible. They are the deeply rooted feelings, thoughts, perceptions and behaviours that individuals cling to, mainly derived from social influences (Hofstede *et al*, 1990) and encompassing religion, background and ethnicity. These assumptions regulate people's realities, perceptions and mannerisms, and are difficult to change as they work at the deepest level. This means that not everyone will be susceptible or open to new (group) norms or mind-sets, particularly when these do not conform to their preconceived perceptions of the world.

Other factors known to influence organizational culture include structural mechanisms (ie the hierarchical structures), channels of communication (open and transparent versus closed and opaque), procedures (such as decision-making latitude) and attitudes to time. Organizations tend to operate within certain time parameters, and this is reflected in their cultures. The ways in which people view time depends on cultural variations and their interpretations (Hall, 1984). Individuals from, for example the Middle East or southern Europe will be accustomed to P-time (polychronic time) – the idea that many things can happen at once – and are therefore less confined by time pressures. This contrasts with M-Time (monochromic time) cultures such as the United States, Australia, Britain and northern Europe, where time is seen as critical and the organizational culture is led by time management (eg deadlines, calendars). Cultural differences were also emphasized by Michael Aldous of the LSE, who compared anglophone and Hispanic working practices:

> I have worked in Anglo and Hispanic settings and there are differences about expectations, how you work on a daily basis. In an Anglo-Saxon culture you turn up on time and you work your hours and you are seen

to be working hard – it's the perception that something is being done, whether it actually is or is not, that is very important. Working in Spain, I didn't feel like that; people just come and get on with what they are doing. It is much more important to build relations.

Michael's experience suggests that P-time cultures are more geared towards relationship building and quality of output than M-time working cultures, where the emphasis is on results.

Having provided an overview of how culture is cultivated, the chapter will next describe the different types of organizational cultures, as outlined by Goffee and Jones (1998), and then offer a variant named 'the learning organization'.

Variants of organizational culture

The Double S Cube Model developed by Goffee and Jones (1998) identifies four cultural variants – fragmented, mercenary, networked and communal (see Figure 5.2) – any of which can be negative or positive in impact – and two dimensions – sociability and solidarity – either of which can be high or low.

Sociability reflects the degree of friendliness among members of an organization. In a culture that has high sociability, the environment is one that projects positive morale and, as Hugo Chapman at the British Museum describes it, 'a strong esprit de corps' – although some drawbacks have been associated with sociability; members may, for example, be inclined to develop cliques or sub-cultures (Goffee and Jones, 1998). Sociability is not a problem in itself, but, it can breed problems such as groupthink (see Chapter 4) and divisions among members (eg in-group and out-group, see Chapter 6).

Solidarity, in contrast, is founded upon shared common goals and refers to the degree to which members feel united in working towards a common purpose. Here, relationships are built around work, tasks and goals; personal feelings are put to the side. Members understand the importance of accomplishing their job-related functions. BBC journalist and broadcaster Sian Williams explains how this applies in the world of broadcasting: work is carried out 'cooperatively, otherwise

FIGURE 5.2 Double S Cube

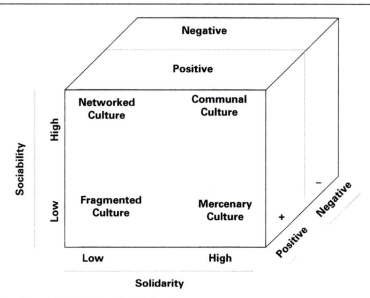

SOURCE: Adapted from Goffee and Jones (1998).

we wouldn't be able to put programmes out. Our communications in news reports have to be brief and to the point. In longer-form programmes there is more room for discussion and engagement.' Working cultures of high solidarity are said to be best suited to environments with a preference for hierarchical structures and clearly prescribed working methods and/or systems. Robert de Vos, flight dispatcher at KLM, gives an example of a situation where systems have been clearly defined. He explains that in his line of work people understand the need to follow prescribed sets of communication measures:

> During the flying operation we have standard procedures and a 'what to say in what situation' protocol (mostly abnormal/emergency situations), and in general we're trained to communicate in a clear and positive manner with each other while maintaining a certain essential hierarchy in the team. In our company we have an '*escalatie*' [escalation] procedure where people communicate situations or any necessary information to their superior, who in turn passes this information on to the next person up in the line. Especially in situations where emotions are involved, this is a way to eliminate that emotional factor while keeping lines of communication in a big company clear.

Mercenary cultures are characterized by a low degree of sociability and a high degree of solidarity. This culture type is results-driven, with a focus on performance. Performance is measured on output alone, with an emphasis on 'winning'. The work ethic is one of long hours, competitiveness and brief communications. Working practices are virtual, non-visible or carried out behind closed doors. Individuals do share certain affinities (generally task-related) but relations will to some extent be cultivated for personal gain.

Communal cultures are high in both sociability and solidarity. Workers tend to get along on both a personal and a professional level. Members tend to identify strongly with organizational values and belief systems. The culture in this variant emphasizes relations and task-related functions. Typical of communal cultures is a high degree of openness in communication and information sharing.

Networked cultures have high sociability and low solidarity and function well in thriving environments (eg Google, Apple, Microsoft and Facebook). They are designed to help people socialize, so such cultures like to create social and open-plan spaces. The aim is to foster better relations and teamwork and to improve the flow of communications through social meaning (Lee and Brand, 2005). This is well depicted by Microsoft Chief Envisioning Officer Dave Coplin, who states:

> Because they want the organization to be more productive, companies like Microsoft and Google and lot of the tech companies create a playful environment because they want people to stay in the office and they want the people developing great code. They want to make work a warm, inclusive space, so some companies provide free restaurants or games areas... also to give them that cognitive diversity, if you like, so people are not sat in front of the screen all day, they get to do lots of different things – and that keeps them fresh in their approach, it keeps the creativity coming in.

Another keen supporter of breaking down barriers is Lewis Pullen, who explains his views on the relationship between culture and physical space: 'We've gone to an open-plan – six months ago I had an oak-panelled office plus a PA's office, and we could have had 30 people in that space; we now have an open-plan office, and my station is no different from any of my team's. We are more equal and I like it.' Whatever the format, an organization's culture remains a reflection of how the organization responds to personal space, density, proximity, layout and hierarchy. While Dave Coplin acknowledges the benefits of open planning, he also offers the flipside saying:

> An interesting dynamic... takes over, especially in an open-plan. What you see a lot in open-plan offices, it's kind of like a herd of animals in the Savannah – completely exposed, vulnerable – and they live in this state of hyper-adrenalized stress because they feel vulnerable. If you look at most open-plan offices what you see is the herd of workers... with their screens facing outward so that anybody can see what they are doing at any point. And what happens to creativity? None of the herd want to break away from the herd, making them even more vulnerable – even in ad agencies and so on, nobody really wants to come up with a really different idea and be picked out by a predator, so people play safe – they do things they all do together. We are killing creativity.

This 'herding of animals' analogy is similar to the concept of deindividuation, which occurs 'when decisions in a group result in a loss of self' (Friedkin, 1999: 856) and aspects of groupthink, unanimity and conformity (see Chapter 4) take centre stage. While the open-plan culture is still in its infancy, and for the most part undefined, new sets of protocols may well be needed to accommodate the different needs of people who work in them. Since a variety of problems have been identified with relation to privacy and density (De Croon *et al*, 2005), noise pollution (Leaman and Bordass, 2005) and interruptions (Craig, 2010), it may be that, in the meantime, workers need to collectively negotiate mutually agreed rules, rituals and boundaries for this relatively new 'boundary-less' working culture.

In contrast to the types discussed above, fragmented cultures are characterized by low solidarity and low sociability; individuals work independently, often behind closed doors. In fragmented cultures, individuals have little contact with one another and do not identify strongly with the organization. Mostly, work carried out is for the benefit of the individual rather than of the organization.

Goffee and Jones (1998) point out that none of the four proposed cultural variants is better or worse than any other. In some instances, organizations can have multiple variants or sub-cultures, or even shift between one and another. In each quadrant there is a potential for cultures to move from a positive to a negative and vice versa, with associated changes and attitudes.

Organizational culture is important because it provides a platform for the way we behave and respond at work. The idea that strong cultures maintain stability and heightened performance presents an interesting problem. Stronger cultures are less open to change and are at risk of breeding conformity, which Dauber, Fink and Yolles (2012) argue makes them more sceptical of internal and/or external triggers. Despite what the culture concept ordinarily stands for – that is, 'stability' – successful organizations recognize that when competing in global and knowledge-intensive environments, their survival is in part determined by their plasticity (see for example Lawson and Samson, 2001). This means a culture will be more successful if it has the flexibility to adjust working practices, is able to accept changes in the nature of jobs, and can adapt to changing and technologically innovative environments. This brings us to the fifth culture variant, the 'learning organization'.

The learning organization

For an organization to learn, it must be receptive to new information and knowledge (Luthans, 1995). In addition, organizations must be able to 'sense, monitor, and scan significant aspects of their environments and relate this information to the operating norms that guide system behaviour' (Morgan, 1998: 77). These attributes define what are referred to as learning organizations (Pedler, 1995; Senge, 1990), and are considered fundamental in preparing members of the organization for the uncertainties of the future. In doing so, learning organizations instil a culture that focuses on continuing transformation and ongoing improvements that keep them up to date with their immediate surroundings both internally and externally. In facilitating this process, learning must take place at three levels: team, organizational and individual. Team and organizational learning revolve around the mechanisms that allow a team to work effectively as an entity. This means agreed systems are in place that encourage learning both in and outside the team, collective thinking, problem-solving and other team-related behaviours that help teams develop, as discussed in Chapter 3. At the individual level, learning takes the form of job-related learning, task learning, continuous professional development and/or reflective learning. The latter comes about through the practice of self-reflection.

To accommodate such practices, says Chris Butt, CEO of Cognisess, learning cultures must strive to be 'open, collaborative dynamic, reflective and analytical'. This raises self-awareness and allows individuals the scope to reflect upon past events, or to revisit and test out current belief systems. However, this can only happen if the culture embraces the unknown, creates a trusting ambience in which members do not feel threatened (for example when mistakes are made, unless these are fundamentally irreversible or the result of inappropriate behaviour). On the subject of potential slips, what is important, Hugo Chapman says, is how these are managed:

> I regard as a good boss somebody who will stand by the person they work with... It is difficult to put into words, it's just an attitude. If my superior starts to criticize somebody who works in my department, I won't leave them exposed, I will be there for them and shoulder the blame with them and I will not just sort of say 'no', point my finger and say 'it is their fault.'

The point is that an open culture where workers can continue to grow and are treated decently (and supported when mistakes are made) will harvest trust and enhance job satisfaction. Cultures where support or care is not fostered will produce the opposite: unhealthy working atmospheres.

Properties of organizational culture

Visible signs of unhealthy organizational cultures include low staff morale and high levels of absenteeism (Gilbreath and Benson, 2004) and turnover. These may arise for several reasons. When organizations have gone through a merger, restructuring or downsizing exercise, for example, it can sometimes leave a bitter taste for those left behind:

feelings of uncertainty (about their own job security perhaps) or feelings of loss (broken friendships with colleagues who have been made redundant). In extreme cases, members project feelings of worthlessness, disengagement, lethargy or lack control. Gabriel (2012) calls this unsettling transition organizational 'miasma'. The important point is that successful organizations will recognize these signs, know when staff morale is low, and address the problems accordingly. Organizations that do not respond may lose valuable members of staff. University reader Samantha Faros describes an organization that fails to take account of problems: 'Each year we are asked to complete an online engagement survey. Staff morale is low – the results illustrate this. Yet management choose to ignore it despite dissatisfaction among workers.' Irrespective of the organizational context, it is important to recognize that culture is always evolving. More importantly, as Chris Butt suggests, there is a need to build 'a positive culture around health and well-being, whether it is providing time off, job shares or counselling. This will lead to less staff turnover, higher productivity and greater successes.'

One model that emphasizes the well-being of staff is Karasek's (1979) Job Demand Control (JDC) Model. The model emphasizes the relationship between job demand and job control and was later extended by adding a third component, resulting in the Job Demand–Control–Support (JDCS) Model (Johnson, Hall and Theorell, 1989; Karasek and Theorell, 1990). The JDCS Model considers three job characteristics – job demands, job control and social support – and outlines the impact these have on job effectiveness (Brough and Pears, 2004), employee motivation and job dissatisfaction. Karasek (1979: 289–90) suggests two components that play a role in work environments: the first is job demands, which include the job requirements and the extent to which workers can decide how to meet them (see Figure 5.3). The second involves job control: that is, a 'working individual's potential control over his task and his conduct during the working day'. Job control, also known as 'decision latitude', relates to the amount of autonomy workers have in making decisions ('decision authority') on the job (Karasek, 1979), the extent of work variety and how far workers are able to use their skills ('skill discretion').

FIGURE 5.3　Job Demand Control model

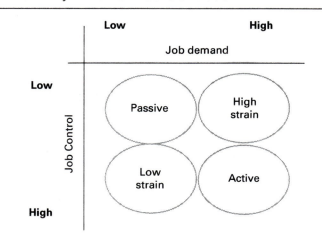

SOURCE: Adapted from Karasek (1979).

Job demand

As previously noted, Karasek and Theorell's (1990) JDCS Model concludes that poor psychosocial and mental health is caused by high job demands in combination with low job control and low social support (see also De Jonge and Kompier, 1997). Further studies confirm these findings, including burnout and other aspects of psychological distress (Houdmont, Kerr and Randall, 2012; Van der Doef and Maes, 1999; Stansfeld *et al*, 1999) such as depression in workers who lack decision-making authority (Warr, 1990; Mausner-Dorsch and Eaton, 2000). Studies of the social support dimension showed that members who do not receive proper support (eg from their supervisors) were more likely to report poor mental well-being (Escriba-Aguir and Tenias-Burillo, 2004) than workers who received higher levels of support. Industry leader Chris Butt explains that 'companies need to understand the external pressures on people and try and lift some of the load. Doing your job well and handling other pressures in life is difficult for people. Good companies recognize this.' At the same time, he adds: 'We operate in a global market – open for business every hour of the day. Companies in developed nations are under pressure – with an aging population and high unemployment; companies are under pressure and pass some of that pressure on to staff.' According to Maike van der Hooghen of the Dutch MOD, it is simple mathematics: 'If you downsize the staff but keep the same tasks, it is very demanding for an organization. The same work has to be done by fewer people. It is increasingly difficult to prioritize and there is more pressure.' Simon Lloyd, HR Director at Santander UK, observes that 'society as a whole is more demanding, customers are more demanding,' and that this is reflected in organizations. He concludes: 'I think that organizations do put more demands on the staff. I do not think that they choose to do this; they do it to deal with the pressures that are put on them.' Guy Lootens of Novotel explains:

> I can certainly see a difference from 10 years ago in what people now have to do – not so much the waiters but more the managers – my front office manager, food and beverage manager, the accounting officer and so on. What they have to do more and more is match what our competitors are offering.

Guy adds: 'There is more and more stress because of what our shareholders demand, and that is depressing because the shareholders are in control.' Peter Stevenhagen of Leiden University has also noticed a shift in job demands:

> When I got my first real job, I was an assistant professor and it was clear what you were supposed to do: teaching, writing papers and giving lectures. Nowadays, if you come in on a tenure track, they also want you to acquire your own funding in various ways, so you spend a lot of times writing proposals. I think proposal writing has become a real industry these days, whereas it was really insignificant 25 years ago.

This is also true for London-based university reader Samantha Faros who explains: 'Academics are asked to do more and more admin, report writing, Excel spreadsheets and grant applications. So yes, I think it is true that the workloads of academics are changing as well as increasing.'

This is confirmed by Joris Luyendijk, former Middle East correspondent for NRC Handelsblad, who affirms: 'In journalism certainly [there are] higher demands and less tolerance because the business model has collapsed and we need to come up with something new. Advertising revenue has migrated to the web, where space costs maybe 1 per cent of what it did on paper.' Meanwhile Ward Edmonds, manager at TrateMedia, explains:

> In the broadcasting business the increasing demands are usually in the form of more output (product) for less time. But the nature of that productivity is changing – with Youtube and Twitter *et al* as rivals, traditional broadcasters are asking their staff to react as fast as those media do. Whereas previously a reporter might do one TV story every few days, now they are expected to do so on a daily basis and provide mega-data online – *and* provide text for the web portal and provide Tweets etc for their followers.

While agreeing that 'more demands are placed on subordinates by management,' he makes clear that 'TrateMedia is a consultancy – we don't accept work if the deadlines are unacceptable/unachievable,' and claims that demands are kept within realistic parameters for both management and their staff. At Wednesday too, demands seem to be sensibly monitored, from client director Allana Brindal's account:

> If you see someone's stressed and needs support, actually removing them from the situation or making sure that they've got an additional pair of hands to help out on a project or making them feel supported is crucial. I think people feel protected in the sense that we won't let a problem go on too long before we do something about it.

The type of work demand Allana describes is sometimes referred to as 'quantitative work overload' (Greenberg and Baron, 2000), which just means excess work. This can make it difficult for individuals to complete their work on time. Recognizing this has created a safety net for Wednesday's workers, as Allana explains:

> We've got a timesheet system, so we run reports at the end of each month and if anybody seems to be working over 100 per cent capacity (which happens quite a lot)... if anyone's consistently pushing over eight hours a day, then they are working way beyond their capacity – that's a red flag where we can sit down and talk about getting freelancers in. We don't want exhausted staff.

This shows that Wednesday is in sync with the approach of JDC's social support dimension (Karasek and Theorell, 1990; Escriba-Aguir and Tenias-Burillo, 2004), realizing that high levels of support contribute to positive well-being and, according to Allana, 'making sure that staff are happy'.

Taking a different point of view, Michael Aldous wonders whether it is 'more the demands on people in terms of the time or in terms of what they are expected to do'. Taking it to the next level, he says:

> Working as a business historian and looking at people working in the 19th century, it does not seem that it was a particularly easy or different [time]. They had heavy workloads, with little protection in terms of labour regulations. So I'm not convinced by people who say they are working longer hours today. Demands in terms of the type of work that you are doing may be different. Maybe the nature of work is changing and what people are expected to do changes; in terms of the amount of time that people have to give, I am not convinced that it is significantly different.

It is interesting to note here that job demands manifest themselves in two ways. When members lack mental stimulation because they are doing repetitive and routine tasks, this is referred to as qualitative job under-load. This contrasts with demands that lead to quantitative work under-load – that is, when employees have too little to do – which also causes problems. Both of these can lead to boredom and demotivation and damage job satisfaction.

On the subject of demands, some of our interviewees also raised the issue of technology. Considering the way technology affects work, L'Oréal HR Director Isabelle Minneci further explains it is not the demands per se that have changed, but rather their content:

> In any organization, everything is getting faster. New technologies and flexible working are increasing the level of interaction and speed for everyone. At L'Oréal, we work in an environment where innovation is key and so the time-to-market to launch new products is critical. The complexity of tasks performed by any individual has increased. A typical marketing role now involves dealing not only with traditional media but also digital and social media environments. This requires new and additional skills. The work demand is therefore not increasing as such but becoming different, faster, more complex. This requires more agile, digitally savvy and efficient staff.

Simon Lloyd has a similar view: 'The growth and use of technology has not made life any simpler or created any more time for people; it has actually made life more demanding.' The demands of technology were also illustrated by Allana Brindal:

> My industry has hardly been hit by the economy's downturn but I do think technology definitely means you have to spin more plates than perhaps you had to in the past... my phone has my e-mail and my work e-mail on it now, and it's switched on all the time, I never switch off – I'm expected to respond to e-mails at all hours; it's not just like I walk away from my work at 6pm and that's it. Clients expect it... because they're paying you to execute a project and they want to know that you're there, and because a lot of our clients are in Europe and the States and they're operating on different time zones, they've got to feel like they've got a local agency.

In journalism, explains Joris Luyendijk, 'Technology is now changing so fast we can hardly keep up – not just the technology we work with but also the technology our audiences use. I'd say tech people these days are more important in newspapers than journalists.'

Peter Stevenhagen also felt that 'the distinction between work and private life has always been pretty blurred', yet at the same time technology 'makes work more productive, in the sense that it is easier to set things up and make things happen these days. Thirty years ago there wasn't even e-mail, so you had to call people up or write a letter. That's quite different from what you can do now over e-mail.'

Lewis Pullen shares similar thoughts: 'I think technology is a double-edged sword... [It] means that you can get across a lot of information and communicate more effectively... but the technology also makes your job harder as the world is changing so fast.' He admits: 'I think there is a lot of pressure on productivity and efficiency because we are now in a global marketplace. So productivity has to be world competitive, and this does put a lot of pressure on people.' He notes that although 'technology has delivered a much easier process, releases people to do what they are good at... which is interact and deliver a better level of personalized service... it never will replace the people.'

Technology is here to stay, so much so that present working environments can barely function without technological applications.

Ease of access has meant that the world wide web (Berners-Lee and Fischetti, 1999) has now attracted 2,749 million individual web users – 38 per cent of the world population (ITU, 2006–2013). Likewise, UK businesses have expanded their interest in technology. Of the 7,700 UK businesses surveyed in 2012, 43 per cent of businesses incorporated social media forums (eg Facebook and LinkedIn) and another 24 per cent used blogs or a microblog like Twitter, while 15 per cent use multimedia content-sharing websites such as Flickr and YouTube (ONS, 2013).

In fact, adds Dave Coplin at Microsoft: 'There is so much more we can do with technology; if we do not change and evolve we are just not going to get to the place that we need to be as a society, as a company or as individuals.' Further statistical predictions suggest an upward trend, with more and more nations gaining greater accessibility, whether in the Americas, Africa, Asia or the Asia-Pacific (ITU, 2006–2013). Worldwide, mobile users currently stand at 6.835 million (ITU, 2006–2013). In Great Britain alone, the Office for National Statistics found that the number of adult computer users in 2013 had increased to 70 per cent, compared with 45 per cent in 2006 (ONS, 2013). In 2013, computer usage among different age groups was assessed, with the highest level (at 88 per cent) found among 16- to 24-year-olds and the second largest those aged 25–34, at 84 per cent. among 35- to 44-year-olds the percentage stood at 80 per cent, closely followed by 45- to 54-year-olds at 76 per cent and 55- to 64-year-olds at 67 per cent. Those over 65 also reported increased computer use, at 37 per cent, compared with 9 per cent in 2006.

Outside the employment sphere, 16 to 34-year-olds are considered by the ONS (2013) as the biggest group engaging in internet activities, with 93 per cent using social networking sites such as Facebook and Twitter, exploring wikis (60 per cent), downloading software (55 per cent) and using the internet as a means for face-to-face conversations through the use of video/webcams (40 per cent). On the topic of technology users, Dave Coplin was clear that while generational differences were apparent in the ways technologies are utilized:

> I do not buy the myth that this is just about kids and young people –
> yes, young people are using technology more innovatively and are much

more open to using technology, but they have an impact on the other generations that they engage with. Whether it is at work or with their parents, it all has a knock-on effect. I think everyone is engaged to some level with technology.

From a different perspective, professor of surgery and former Head of Department at University Hospital Caen Guy Samama argues:

I can speak only in my field. In the field of diagnosis students are less and less clever, less and less intelligent because they believe more and more in the technology, so they now move quickly from the symptoms to the diagnostic results of the MRI scan. They believe in these results, they all take it at face value.

While technology – rightly or wrongly – dominates our workplace, the real question is: what will become of people who are overwhelmed by technological demands? The question was put to Chris Butt, who replied:

We have formed new habits. I check my e-mail morning and night; it has become automatic. Software companies are active 24 hours a day, seven days a week. It is a real issue, it comes back to self-reflection. [It is a problem] if you do not acknowledge that you are doing this, and it comes back to control – whether you can control your habits and actually break them. Some people are naturally able to do that well. It comes back down to being valued – if you can communicate and have been contacted, it makes you feel valued and there is a sense of rush that you so desire at a brain level. It is difficult to turn that off when you are getting it; there is a flip side when it is negative.

With this being a relatively new area of research, the psychological and/or physical effects of using technology, both in and outside work, have yet to be understood. According to Christ Butt: 'Technology is an element that we need to get good at and keep up with. I don't think we know... yet, whether it has had an impact on emotional development, empathy and cognitive function; some of the effects are probably positive and some not.' There are questions involving the effects of regular exposure to non-face-to-face communication media (eg Twitter, message boards/walls, chat rooms, Facebook, MySpace) and how they impact proficiency in communication. It remains to be seen how regular exposure to such media can lead to (mis)interpretation of real-life non-verbal cues, and the impact this could have on human rapport-building. Didier Souillat at Hakkasan shares similar concerns, saying: 'It is all about this virtual world we live in, all about instant communication with people we do not see. So people can operate these devices very well but they are not good face-to-face communicators. It is going to be a problem.' It is vital to find answers to the questions surrounding technological communication and engagement, as employers need recruits who have appropriate interpersonal and communication skill sets. In most jobs, this is a key requirement.

Job control

Despite the finding that low control over how work is to be done, coupled with high job demands and low social support, is linked to job dissatisfaction (Karasek and Theorell, 1990), traditional command control cultures are still prevalent across many types of organization. Dave Coplin emphasizes this: 'We still have this command control culture in what we do, and I think the biggest barrier for most organizations is that you have to let go of that control.' It is better, says Pat Joseph, if we adopt a more 'hands off' approach. In doing so:

> The best thing to do is to employ people who are better than you. Then you do not have to worry about what they are doing so you do not have to micro-manage them, which means that you start trusting people; and if you start trusting people you get the best out of them. They feel empowered and responsible and they make their own decisions.

Ultimately, this would suggest a win–win all round. So, why do organizations exercise control? For Peter Stevenhagen it is a mystery:

> Once people have earned tenure in a maths research institute or education institute, they should be offered the right kind of position, not spend their time on a multitude of bureaucratic procedures that are part of a show run by a legion of managers and bureaucrats. This is also a matter of trust, and typically the current attitude of academic managers all the way up to the government and ministry of education is that they want to procedurally define every aspect of academic life. I think if you are a professional you should be able to count on simply being trusted to do this.

Peter argues that subordinates should be entrusted with the work they have been commissioned to do rather than being dictated to about 'how' it must be done. It seems Peter is not alone. London-based university reader Samantha Faros describes similar problems in her sector: 'These days we are much more micro-managed; workloads are numerically calculated, right down to a T. This I think is totally unnecessary. What needs to be developed is greater trust between senior management and employees.' This can be achieved if organizations adopt a more decentralized approach, and empower workers by giving them more control and greater decision-making latitude. Yet, explains Dave Coplin, 'the challenge is to give the leader/manager the confidence to let go of the control – it is a personality thing, but it also comes down to the power you hold within the organization.' An insightful glimpse into Marine operations is provided by Alan Litster:

> We explain our intent very, very carefully to our people, and the higher headquarters will tell somebody what to do, not *how* to do it. How he is going to do it will very much be his business... What we try to engender is the philosophical basis of how we do command and control and we call this 'mission command'. We will plan in as much detail as we can to the very lowest level, we will rehearse as often as we can, so that [even if the radio link to HQ breaks down], people will look at their watch and know 'I should be doing this now' and they will not wait to be told. We will do what is called a 'Rehearsal of Concept Drill': we will use a map or a model and maybe tin cans on a board, and at the very lowest level we will ask our Marines to almost repeat the plan back to us: 'If this happens I know I am going to do this. If somebody is injured here, I know that is where we are going to get the helicopter to pick him up. I know if that piece of equipment breaks down, this is the plan to get it moved.'

This 'mission command' approach triggered thoughts of whether similar processes could be applied to organizational life. The question was put to Alan Litster, who pointed out a problem:

> Your life depends on the plan working in the military. If a business plan goes wrong, you might have to explain yourself to the chief financial officer or chief executive and you might have an uncomfortable meeting, but in our line of work you are writing a deeply personal letter

to someone's parents telling them why their son is dead. Our ethos is tremendously important to us because of what underpins it, and this is very hard for a civilian company to replicate. People are prepared to die for my organization, but I am not sure that people are prepared to die for Microsoft.

While it is true that Marine life is a far cry from the everyday office environment, what nonetheless resonates is their clearly defined culture of organization, attention to detail and the thought given to contingency planning. Alan demonstrates this further in saying that: 'We also ensure continuity of command; there is always someone who can do the leader's job, so that if the leader gets shot there is always someone who can step up and take his place.' What was perhaps most striking was Alan's sense of commitment and the strong work ethic that formed this unique working culture, where the message is clearly communicated to all its members: 'Our ethos is our business and our people.'

The message that organizations are over-managed and under-led is getting through to some. In keeping with the views of Karasek (1979) and Marquardt (2002), both of whom refer to the importance of high job control, Dave Coplin describes how 'Microsoft gives me the tools and technology but most importantly instils a culture that says: "Dave, we do not care where you are, what you are doing, how you do your work, as long as those things get done". What this means for me as an individual – it's so empowering.' At Wednesday, Client Director Allana Brindal affirms that individuals are empowered to make their own decisions, describing the culture as:

> ... a very open environment in comparison to other agencies I've worked at, where if you kind of arrive a bit late, you feel like someone's going to be marking you down on a piece of paper, whereas at Wednesday it's quite professional: you rock up whenever you want because it's acknowledged you'll get the work done and you'll stay as long as it takes to get it done... You don't feel like you're at school where the bell's ringing and you've got to be sitting at your desk.

Dave Coplin adds:

> What Microsoft actually does is trust me as an individual to be professional. It is for me to keep the promises I have made and do all

the things that I am supposed to do, and that is a huge leap of faith for some organizations. This is a massively different work culture from the world that we have come from.

Empowerment was also cited by Didier Souillat: 'those people you are hiring, you have to empower them to do what they have been hired to do and you have to give the people the tools to do their jobs properly.' Borja Manchado agrees: 'I like to enable people to do things, instead of directing them to do what I think is best.' Giving decision-making leverage to members not only leads to strengthened organizational commitment but will also enhance people's confidence in feeling part of the overall decision-making process.

Decision-making plays an important role in influencing organizational direction, and a variety of factors (see Chapters 2 and 4) have been known to interfere with decision-making, including risk-taking behaviours (Shapira, 1995) and emotions (Parducci and Fabre, 1995). Kahn and Isen (1993) suggest that positive emotions lead to variety-seeking behaviour, while Bodenhausen, Sheppard and Kramer (1994) point out that negative emotions are more likely to fuel stereotypical thinking and mean that people will be less open to new ideas. Decision-making practices remain complex; what may seem a good decision for one organization may be wrong for others. Sometimes, says Lewis Pullen, decision-making involves 'making hard decisions – not popular decisions but hard ones'. For example, the decision to make redundancies may be necessary for the financial survival of an organization, but at the same time will trigger feelings of insecurity or decreased morale for those left behind: the organizational 'miasma' described earlier. Alan Litster remarks that: 'You have to make some quite harsh decisions, but leadership in military life is not a popularity contest.' In all, decision-making is inherent to organizational life, and – for better or worse – affects the entire organization. In facilitating effective decision-making, Drucker (1967) suggests six steps are followed in the decision-making practices (see Figure 5.4).

First off, it is important to identify the type of decision people are asked to make. According to Drucker there are two types of decision-making: 'generic', when a familiar situation recurs, and 'unique', when problems are managed individually or pragmatically. In brief, the first step involves classifying the problem. The second step is to

FIGURE 5.4   Six-step decision-making process

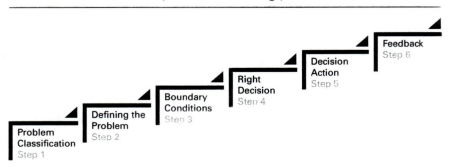

SOURCE: Adapted from Drucker (1967).

define it: that is, to identify the key issues. The third step concerns boundary conditions, making clear what the decision must accomplish: in other words, clarifying the goals. Step four involves asking whether the chosen decision will meet all the boundary conditions. The fifth step is to convert the decision into action. Drucker stipulates that it is often here that post-decision-making processes fail, because there is no follow up or process in place to convert the decision into action. To avoid dilution and to facilitate the decision practice, follow-up questions must be asked. For example: Who in the organization needs to be informed of the decision? What has to be done so that people can take the action? Learning cultures, as discussed earlier have the capacity to reflect on past decision-making, in particular when decisions have produced poor results. This type of feedback is about revisiting the decision that was made and deciding whether the right course was taken, making this the sixth step.

Vroom and Jago (1988) also provide a useful framework to facilitate decision-making practices between managers and their subordinates. In their view five decision-making styles are used to facilitate leader decision-making. In brief, the model provides a two-way platform: first, based on the given information, it assists leaders in deciding how to solve potential problems; second, it provides a set of questions for leaders to identify the best course of action and how best to work with subordinates. At Novotel, Guy Lootens believes it is important to involve employees. He describes how they do this: 'If decisions involve staff then we put our preliminary proposal on the staff canteen notice board. Staff can respond over a one-week period. We discuss their responses at our next meeting and the final decision is then presented on paper.'

Conclusion

This chapter has provided an overview of the different types of organizational culture, including the construct of learning organizations. Each culture is unique and is marked by differing symbols, rituals and artefacts. The chapter suggests that culture is best constructed through the joint efforts of all members, though it recognizes the role leaders play in driving culture. It is recommended that culture should be founded upon moral and ethical principles that set precedents for how people should behave towards one another. Job satisfaction is influenced by job demands, controls and decision-making latitude. Successful organizations recognize the importance of employee well-being and, in doing so, cultivate a culture of care, support, trust and empowerment (see Chapter 7). It is suggested that when all these variables are in place, this is likely to boost morale. The survival of organizations will depend on their leadership (see Chapter 7) and degree of resilience, flexibility and receptiveness in responding to internal and external events. This sets the stage for Chapter 6, in which an overview will be presented of the different leadership theories.

Leadership

This chapter introduces the concept of leadership and outlines a number of the better-known paradigms and how leadership theory as we know it has evolved. The main purpose is to illustrate the essential features in effective leadership, each of which will be described. To simplify this journey, the key leadership theories have been categorized into six taxonomies: Trait Theory (Stogdill, 1948), Style Theory (Lewin, Lippitt and White, 1939), Behavioural Theory (Fleishman, 1953), Contingency Theory (Fiedler, 1967), Situational Theory (Hersey and Blanchard, 1988) and Leader–Member Exchange Theory (Graen and Uhl-Bien, 1995). The chapter will also offer insights from industry leaders and their views on what is considered effective leadership. The chapter starts with a brief overview of the psychological underpinnings of leadership theory.

Leadership theories

The main questions that drive leadership theory are 'What is leadership?' and 'What is considered effective leadership?' The first focuses on the examination of what leaders do and looks at how leaders become more effective. The second focuses on leadership, exploring its processes and relationships to differing workplace situations. To the first, Argyris (1983) emphasizes a need to strengthen partnerships between leaders and their followers, while industry leader Roland Esnis, Department Manager at IBM France, talks about the importance of 'leading by example' which, he says, 'instils a culture of commitment, solidarity and recognition'. Linda DeGrow, former general manager at Voith Industrial Services Inc, says a leader should be 'decisive, [someone] who can calmly navigate the team through a storm, with good listening skills and good problem-solving skills – someone who can act as a change agent'. On the subject of what constitutes leadership, Burns (1978) believes leadership is about setting a moral example. Taking leadership to a different and higher level, Chris Butt, CEO of Cognisess, states that

> Good leadership is about understanding your own limits; if you can bring people around you who are really competent and can fill in the bits that you cannot do. Not everyone can do everything, so it is about knowing that. Poor leadership is where you try to do too much and you do not build a team around you.

Managing Director of Hakkasan, Didier Souillat echoes similar ideas, suggesting that good leaders create 'an association of talents, and leadership – in this case making sure you have got enough talent around you that complements you'.

With regard to the question of what constitutes leadership, researchers agree on two points: first, that leadership is perceived as a universal phenomenon across different cultures, heritages and geographies; second, that leadership is fundamental to organizational life and that effective leadership is vital for effective organizations. Without strong leadership, organizations are less likely to thrive, the workforce will be dissatisfied and the organization will stagnate. However, where researchers disagree is about what leadership is. A number of theories have been developed to answer this question and to understand which style of leadership is the most successful. While no one specific leadership approach has fully succeeded in offering the best leadership solution for all organizations, this chapter presents the main developments in leadership theories and insights from leaders of industry.

Great man theory

The first leadership theory came to be known as the 'Great Man' theory (Carlyle, 1840) and argues that leaders are born with the 'right stuff', suggesting leadership is innate. The theory also posits that only men become good leaders, and only men 'in great times of need will rise'. While there is no objection against 'man', Great Man theory proves to be not only elitist but also sexist. Somehow the many 'Great Women' of our time appear to have been ignored despite their undoubted influence. Rather, when thinking of historic leaders, there is all too often a tendency to default to male citations and examples of a political, militant, entrepreneurial or spiritual nature.

In view of Carlyle's suggestion that leadership qualities are innate, 32 interviewees were questioned on whether people are born with leadership qualities or whether they are learnt. Of the 32 industry leaders, 10 favoured the innateness perspective (see Table 6.1).

The first to support the innate stance was former Chief System Engineering Manager of the National Theatre Guy Kendall, who states that: 'People are born to lead – so perhaps teaching management is straightforward but the leadership function requires a strong personality

TABLE 6.1   Leadership as nature (N = 10)

Organization	Country	Innate
British Museum	UK	Innate
CHU	France	Innate
Gaucho	UK	Innate
Hakkasan	UK	Innate
KLM	NL	Innate
Mitsubishi Bank	UK	Innate
MOD	NL	Innate
National Theatre	UK	Innate
Royal Marines	UK	Innate
University	UK	Innate

that is surely not taught.' Hugo Chapman, Head of the Prints and Drawings Department at the British Museum, similarly echoes, 'The basic human qualities of leadership are, I think, innate.' Dutch MoD Head of Branch Maike van der Hooghen suggests that: 'A person has to have a certain drive and I think you have to be born with this. Born with a drive to improve things, to take charge and to organize and influence people towards a certain goal.' Similarly, Royal Marine Alan Litster thinks: 'It would be very difficult for you to become a credible leader unless you had some kind of innate quality within you.'

Thus a number of interviewees seem to share Carlyle's view that leadership is an innate predisposition. Yet industry leaders differed from Carlyle in their views on the ways in which leadership is driven, with a focus on expansion rather gender and status. Anthropological explanations have been sought to explain Carlyle's androcentric tone. According to Lerner (1986), it is our longstanding relationship with gender bias. Through extensive research, Lerner was able to pinpoint the causes of male control and dominance, taking her back to Mesopotamia and covering a 2,500-year period from 3100 to 600 BC. Lerner surmised that these forms of oppression act as a classification system that shapes the relations among men and women in how they are perceived. It comes then as no surprise that this long tradition of subordination influenced leadership roles.

Professor of Surgery Guy Samama comments:

> You can cultivate it but if you are not born to be a leader you will not be a good leader. You may be the best surgeon in the world and you may be a good practitioner in your field of expertise but if you are a poor leader, regardless of the quality of your surgery, you will destroy everything else because you are unable to lead your people and build your team.

Robert de Vos agrees: 'You're born with it – you can teach a lot but real leadership you're born with, it's the character of a person and what a person is.'

The view that leadership ability is an innate predisposition gives rise to an interesting debate that we will return to in Chapter 7 with the introduction and novel concept of humanistic leadership. The above views are closely synchronized with the ideas of Trait Theory, which we now turn to.

Trait Theory

The underlying assumption behind trait theories of leadership is that leaders share common traits, which are interpreted here as the characteristics that drive thoughts, feelings and leaders' actions. Particular traits are said to distinguish leaders from their followers. In the lead-up to the Second World War a platform was set in the 1930s for researchers to pursue their interest in leadership. Post-war pioneers include Bird (1940), Jenkins (1947) and Stogdill (1948), whose thinking marks a turning point in the study of trait leadership. Bird identified, from his 27 studies, 79 traits that distinguish leaders from their followers. Later, Bird distilled these further to just four (see Table 6.2).

Jenkins' research findings on leaders were predominantly extracted from the military, and the characteristics he found (eg intelligence, physique, social background and technical competence) may be atypical and seen only in that particular context. Stogdill (1948), meanwhile, used a different sample, one that was non-military. In Stogdill's initial exploration between 1904 and 1947, five clusters emerged (see Table 6.2). In 1970, Stogdill analysed further research and identified six groupings from the 163 studies surveyed. The findings differentiated leaders and non-leaders and effective and ineffective leaders (see

TABLE 6.2 Trait studies

Bird (1940)	Stogdill (1948)	Stogdill (1970)	Lord *et al* (1986)	Kirkpatrick & Locke (1991)
Intelligent	Status	Intelligence	Intelligence	Cognitive ability
Extravert	Responsibility	Personality	Extravert	Drive
Initiative	Capacity	Task-related skills	Dominance	Task knowledge
Humour	Participation	Social background	Adaptability	Motivation
	Achievement	Social characteristics	Conservative	Integrity
		Physical	Masculinity	Confidence

Table 6.2). In studies between 1948 and 1970, Stogdill noticed that certain traits were more visible in leaders than non-leaders though, contrary to earlier findings, Stogdill (1970) concludes it is problematic to isolate traits specific to leaders without considering situational factors, suggesting leaders may have the 'right stuff' for one situation but not for another. Years later, Stogdill's findings were subjected to a meta-analysis by Lord, De Vader and Alliger (1986), who found intelligence, dominance and masculinity stood out as the most prominent of the six leadership traits (see Table 6.2). In 1991, further research by Kirkpatrick and Locke also identified six different traits (see Table 6.2). What these cross-sectional findings illustrate is that there is some degree of overlap in leader traits.

In interviews with industry leaders, the traits they considered essential for effective leadership echoed those identified in the studies of Stogdill (1970), Lord, De Vader and Alliger (1986) and Kirkpatrick and Locke (1991) (see Table 6.3).

For Alan Litster, 'Probably the most important one is judgement. You are also expected to be reliable, intelligent and have the capacity to solve a problem very quickly on your own feet.' For Simon Lloyd, HR Director at Santander UK, 'Leaders must be able to emotionally engage with people, have a vision, communicate, make decisions and

TABLE 6.3   Qualitative data set of the most common leader characteristics perceived by interviewees (N = 32)

Vision	Inclusivity	Listening	Intelligent
Direction	Resilience	Recognition	Caring
Empathy	Decision-making	Feedback	Humour
Engagement	Empower	Judgement	Confident
Communication	Clarity	Reliable	Empathy
Bringing people along	Integrity	Learning	Growth
Inspire	Trustworthy	Cognitive	Self-motivation

be able to take complex and difficult issues and turn them into simple issues and decision-making ability.' For Human Resource Director Isabelle Minneci, 'A true leader is someone who inspires others, conveys enthusiasm and a desire to surpass oneself; has a significant presence and impact on others and exudes self-confidence.' Wednesday's Client Director, Allana Brindal, explains:

> [It means] being super clear with exactly what you're hoping to achieve and engaging people in that kind of conversation. I think having a good sense of humour is really important as well, not taking yourself too seriously, [and] being creative because people respect original thought, the ability to push the boundaries, and I think that confidence is very important.

Yet Chris Butt admits: 'It is a difficult question to answer and one that we will be studying for a long time. I imagine it will be a combination of emotional and cognitive factors, and the ability to learn.'

Theorists and industry leaders agree on certain traits specific to leaders (eg confidence, empowerment, resilience, intelligence, integrity, humour), as these seem to re-emerge across the different studies and interview data sets. While trait theories have given us some benchmarks with which to differentiate leaders from non-leaders, no consistent relationship was found between trait and leader effectiveness (Stogdill, 1974). This may be due to the methodological inconsistencies at the time that the research was carried out. As leadership research was still in its infancy, too few test measurements were readily available, suggesting existing measurements may have impacted validity and reliability. As a result different researchers used different methods that later proved inconsistent. Additionally, researchers disagreed as to what exactly traits signified, which led to variations in how they defined traits. This could also explain the sampling issues: earlier studies recruited mainly low-ranking managers, supervisors or adolescents, so their findings may have been relatively one-sided. Other shortcomings involved neglect in recognizing the complex relationships between leaders and their followers.

While the theory is underpinned by the understanding that traits are stable, identifiable, measurable and transferable, it also asserts (unlike Great Man Theory) that certain traits may prove useful in one situation but not another. It also claims that while leaders may be born with the 'right stuff', this does not mean that they will necessarily be successful. Trait theorists acknowledge that in addition to traits, other factors play a role, and this provides the foundation for style and contingency theories.

Style theory

In response to the trait approach, in the 1940s a new line of thinking emerged. Behaviourist theorists were the first to suggest that leadership is not innate but rather can be learnt. Of a similar opinion, 11 industry leaders interviewed for this book shared this view (see Table 6.4).

TABLE 6.4   Leadership as nurture (N = 11)

Company	Country	Learnt
BBC	UK	Learnt
Four Seasons	Egypt	Learnt
Gielly Green	UK	Learnt
IBM	France	Learnt
L'Oréal	UK	Learnt
Microsoft	UK	Learnt
The Mill	UK	Learnt
Ohad Maoz	Israel	Learnt
Santander	UK	Learnt
Rare Tea Company	UK	Learnt
Wednesday	UK	Learnt

From first-hand experience, Resort Manager Borja Manchado of the Four Seasons Hotel argues:

> Leadership can be taught and it's very important that the people around you give you the right leadership, that you have the right mentors around your career. Many people say you are born as a leader but I don't believe in that. I never felt I was a natural leader; I think I learnt how to become a leader every day.

Shai Greenberg, hair stylist at the hair boutique Gielly Green, believes leadership 'is environmental. Like everything in life, it can be learnt. A true leader should be willing to learn all the time.' Organizational Psychologist Ohad Maoz also considers it is 'something we grow up with, it is formed by our experience – but some are born with it.' Allana Brindal says: 'I don't think that everybody can be great leaders but I do feel there are skill sets that can be learnt.' Meanwhile, Henrietta Lovell, founder of the Rare Tea Company, suggests:

> I believe that it can be taught. You can give people confidence and with this confidence they can lead others. By inspiring people to believe in what they are doing, they can step outside of their job and their personal lives and wants to take others with them on that revolution. The nature of your job and how you approach it can help you become a leader.

Similar ideas are echoed by Microsoft's Chief Envisioning Officer, Dave Coplin: 'I think it can be taught; it is a bit of both but I do believe that it can be taught.' Yet if this were true, it would imply that all leaders could learn to be charismatic and/or inspirational. In response to that thought, Manager Ward Edmonds of TrateMedia JLT surmizes:

> There is such a thing as a 'natural leader' – we've all met them or worked with them. To imply that leadership is only about training and a learnt skill set disregards the crucial elements that pre-exist – what are often referred to as innate. To me it involves communication skills, an ability to empathize (or appear to).

This poses an interesting quandary: while trait theorists argue that traits are stable and impact personality (see Chapter 2), this would imply that leadership could not be learnt. Years later, in support of this idea, developmental psychologists undertook studies into the Theory of Mind (Leslie, 1987), claiming the innateness of certain traits, such as empathy. It was concluded that unless individuals can identify with other peoples' feelings, desires, beliefs and/or viewpoints, empathy is unlikely to be cultivated. This analysis furthers the idea that other deeply rooted traits may in fact be impossible to nurture either (eg integrity, care).

This thought-provoking notion raises the question whether it is worthwhile or fair to push people in senior roles on to leadership development courses, if no training programme can or will effectively develop specific leader traits (eg charisma, empathy or integrity), unless people are predisposed to them. Simon Lloyd, of Santander UK, recognizes, that this 'is something that you are born with – you cannot teach people integrity or ethics'. Effectively this brings us back to the innateness discussion in which, University Reader Samantha Faros affirms: 'Leadership is definitely innate: you cannot teach people integrity or morality, this has to come within. You can coach leaders in how to communicate better but the essential traits that separate leaders from non-leaders, I don't believe can be taught.'

This idea is echoed by Chris Butt, who suggests: 'It is a very different skill set to graduate from manager to leader. So some people do get [over promoted] and are frankly out of their depth and perhaps don't have the ability. So it is about building your talent pool correctly.' It seems Simon and Chris are not alone in thinking this, given that there may well be a deficit right now in leadership talent according to leadership expert and author John Adair. In an interview with Helen Mayson, he stresses that: 'To improve the competence of leaders we need organizations who are willing to think strategically.' Leadership and management degree courses sometimes fail to equip graduates with well-balanced portfolios of 'hard' (ie managerial systems, finance), and 'softer' skill sets. In seeking to answer the question of how we can identify leadership potential, Chris Butt explains:

> From our point of view we want to see if there is a correlation between cognitive, emotional and social attributes. If we can identify what is excellent within an organization with their current leadership profile –

for instance, if someone has been doing particularly well and driving the business forward – we want to understand what this looks like from a neuroscience and psychology perspective.

In a follow-up question I asked Chris: what are the systems that organizations can implement to help nurture this potential? According to Chris: 'They need to know what it looks like and how it fits in with the wider talent pool. Companies should do more "people analytics" – get behind the data to highlight the talent profile, see what trends successful managers and leaders display.' It is this gap that Chris Butt is trying to fill, together with academic and industry associates, through studying the different cognitive and emotional attributes that underpin leadership (for more information on Cognisess, visit **www.cognisess.com**). In the meantime, it appears that not everyone is suitable for leadership roles.

The style theory approach to leadership suggested that leader behaviour could be identified along a continuum of three styles: democratic, autocratic and laissez-faire. The first researchers (Lewin, Lippitt and White, 1939), to develop what became known as style theory were interested in exploring different leader effects on individual and group behaviour. In doing so, the researchers studied 11-year-old boys across four after-school clubs, each of which had been subjected to different styles. This study had a major impact on leadership theory despite having been based on a sample of 11-year-old boys.

Central to the first leadership style, democratic leadership, is the notion of egalitarianism. That is, leaders seek consensus by involving subordinates in decisions. Democratic leaders delegate responsibilities to subordinates and in doing so distribute roles fairly (Cartwright and Zander, 1968). Henrietta Lovell tries to practise egalitarianism by making sure her employees see that she is fair in how the work is shared across her team. She admits:

I do secure many of the most interesting projects but I am also prepared to do the tasks that I set others to do. I [want to be fair] when taking on tasks, so sometimes I take on less prestigious ones so that my team does not feel that there is a big division between us. At the same time, I also try to include them in exciting projects.

Picking up on the notion of egalitarianism, Ward Edmonds raises an important point, explaining how leadership is about finding the right balance and, in doing so, having 'an ability to project a "separateness" between the leader and the cost/price of that leadership'. Similarly, Bill George (2003), author of the book *Authentic Leadership*, explains that leaders who demonstrate egalitarianism and encourage inclusivity are more likely to influence and gain the commitment of those around them. The democratic style is perceived as the most favourable and seems to resonate with most industry leaders, including Chief Marketing Office Lewis Pullen who says: 'At Qantas we want to involve staff in the planning of the business and want to create a sustainable business model.'

Under autocratic rule, leaders are non-transparent and do not involve members in any decision-making practices. Compliance is key, regulated through tight controls and disciplinary measures in the form of either punishments or rewards. This could explain the low levels of group morale found in Lewin, Lippitt and White's study in 1939, and why efforts dropped to a low level when leaders were absent (Lippitt and White, 1943). Typically, leaders who exert a high degree of control leave no space for empowerment or scope for innovation. The subject of control came up repeatedly in the interview with Dave Coplin, 'I think the biggest barrier for most organizations is you've got to let go of that control. The challenge now is to move towards a style of leadership that encourages creativity and empowers people to be really innovative in how they achieve those outcomes.' Dave went on to say:

> We want to manage less and lead more. A good leader will establish the context of the outcome that the organization is trying to achieve, make sure that everybody understands the overall goal of the organization, then help the individuals collectively and individually figure out the best way to achieve that outcome

Dave believes Microsoft are ahead of the game, affirming that 'there is a huge difference in the way that we see things going forward' – a far cry from the traditional command and control approaches to leadership.

Characteristics of the laissez-faire leader represent the unhappy medium of neither extremity. For the most part leaders are 'wishy washy' and disseminate responsibility; in worst-case scenarios they abdicate the leader role. The laissez-faire leader neither sets goals, commits, communicates, provides feedback nor shares information (Goodnight, 2004). Leaders who adopt this style are incapable of driving teams forward and instead rely heavily on the goodwill of subordinates to get results.

In evaluating leadership style theory, a number of observations can be made. The knowledge that leadership styles first had been identified from observation of 11-year-old boys raises the question of whether different findings might have arisen if the sample population had consisted of professional adult workers. Results also showed that under autocracy, greater hostility was projected towards the leader and between group members, yet does not explain why this may be. Also it has been shown that participants under autocratic rule tend to be much quicker to solve problems than participants exposed to a democratic style of leadership (eg Shaw, 1955). It is unclear whether this is due to time constraints or the pressure to perform. As for the laissez-faire approach, researchers concluded that it generated the lowest productivity levels. While space does not permit an in-depth review of the literature, it would be fair to say that leadership style does in some shape or form influence how people approach work. Despite the discrepancies, Lewin's ideas formed a successful backdrop for future business settings in which democratic leadership was deemed useful in fostering and developing cohesive working environments, motivation and subordinate satisfaction.

Behaviour Theory – The Ohio Studies

About the same time, and in parallel with Lewin's (1939) studies, in 1945 the Bureau of Business Research at Ohio State University (Fleishman and Harris, 1962) conducted a renowned series of leadership studies. The aim was to examine subordinate perceptions of leader behaviour and leaders' self-perceptions of their own behaviour. Different cohorts were sampled, ranging from manufacturing supervisors, Navy department Air Force commanders, bomber crews, college students and their administrators. The researchers developed and used the Leader Behaviour Description Questionnaire (LBDQ) to assess leader behaviour in a number of different situations. The questionnaire contained 150 items in which subordinates were asked to rate how well and how often people in leadership positions operated in their leadership role (Fleishman, 1953). The items were categorized into nine dimensions: integration, communication, production, representation, fraternization, organization, evaluation, initiation and domination (Fleishman, 1953). The results pointed towards two behavioural dimensions and four styles (see Figure 6.1).

FIGURE 6.1   Four-Quadrant Model

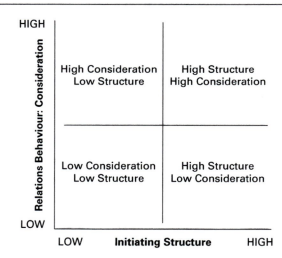

SOURCE: Adapted from the Ohio Studies.

From the research, two behavioural dimensions emerged. The first, named 'consideration' – also known as 'person-orientated' – characterizes a leader who is relationship driven. The second behavioural dimension, 'initiating structure' – also referred to as 'task-orientated' – is the degree to which the leader directs subordinates towards tasks. Fleishman (1973) concluded that effective leadership was directly correlated with 'high consideration' and 'high initiating structure' (see Figure 6.1). Making the case against the restrictive methods of scientific management, the Ohio study proved valuable in laying the foundation for leaders to practice both task and relationship-orientated behaviour. It was suggested that this combination would boost team morale, encourage greater commitment and reduce absenteeism (Fleishman, Harris and Burtt, 1955). In addition to these illuminating findings, the researchers recognized one further component that would influence the style of leadership: that is, the context in which the leader works.

Behaviour Theory – The Michigan Studies

At about the same time, researchers from the Survey Research Centre at the University of Michigan (Katz, Maccoby and Morse, 1950) also took an interest in leadership studies. Results pointed towards three behavioural styles, two (task and person orientated) in parallel with the Ohio studies. The first dimension, 'task-oriented behaviour', focuses on the division of tasks where leaders organize, plan and coordinate activities to ensure members are clear about what needs doing and have the resources to do it. The second dimension is 'relationship-oriented behaviour', which centres on relationship building. The third dimension that emerged from the findings is the 'participative behavioural style'. Here, leaders adopt a number of strategies to ensure all members (individual and group) actively participate. Methods include regular team meetings that provide a platform for idea sharing and group decision-making, and assist in problem-solving. The idea behind participative leadership is that leaders act in a more consultative manner. Lewis Pullen advocates this, providing a glimpse of the working practices of Qantas: 'It is now evolving into a strong consultative culture where we are inclusive'; he admits, however, that: 'It's interesting, the balance between [being] consultative and actually providing direction, as people do want to be led. Getting this balance right is a very interesting challenge.' Hugo Chapman suggests that sometimes leadership is 'about taking people places that they do not necessarily want to go, but you persuade them'. Sometimes boundaries become blurred, as a fine line emerges between what is considered just and what is not. Cultures that seek genuine participation by their sub-ordinates show good intent, while others pay lip service to it. Samantha Faros is emphatic about this: 'It is nothing but pretence; we are asked to take part in all sorts of consultations, but really we know it is simply a tick-boxing exercise. Most decisions are made at executive level way before staff is supposedly involved.' Participation is further dissected by Allana Brindal, who describes 'being really engaged with what people are saying and at meetings and contributing, but not feeling the need to talk over everyone. I will say something when I have something to contribute, not because I feel like I need to steal the limelight.' She adds: 'I think it's much more respectful to be quiet until you have something to say and that definitely harvests respect.'

In summary, both studies proved a milestone in the field of organizational behaviour. Initial studies saw the dimensions 'initiating structure' and 'consideration' at opposite ends of a single continuum, though later studies revealed that the two dimensions could be regarded as independent and thus occur simultaneously. Research reported positive correlations between participation and job satisfaction, in particular when subordinates were given decision-making latitude. For the first time since the Hawthorne Studies (see Chapter 1), leaders were urged to engage in more 'person-orientated' behaviour and reflect upon their relationships with subordinates. This laid the foundation for future theories, including the Leadership Grid by Blake and Mouton (1964).

Leadership Grid

Building on the Ohio and Michigan studies, Blake and Mouton (1964) delivered a framework for leaders to assess their leadership behaviour and attitude. The Leadership Grid (previously named the Managerial Grid) represented two dimensions: the vertical dimension represents 'concern for people' and the horizontal dimension 'concern for production' (see Figure 6.2). Blake and Mouton (1964) claim that on either dimension leaders can score anywhere from (1.1) to a maximum score of (9.9). Leaders can use their scores on the grid to help determine their behavioural style. The grid proposes five distinct leadership styles: authoritarian (9.1), country club (1.9), impoverished (1.1), middle of the road (5.5) and team leader (9.9).

Leaders who use an authoritarian style believe that employees are 'simply a means to an end'. Employees are exposed to stringent controls, rules and procedures, with a preferred culture of rivalry. This is done

FIGURE 6.2 Leadership grid

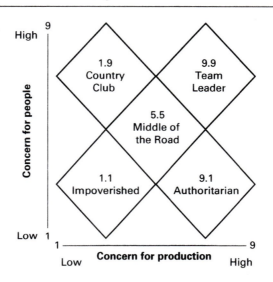

SOURCE: Adapted from Blake and Mouton (1964).

to ensure members outperform each other and serves as a mechanism for leaders to implement measures of punishment with the aim of enforcing compliance (ie normative social influence – see Chapter 4). Effectively, authoritarian leaders show low concern for people and high concern for production. On the grid this will equate to a score of 9.1. This style corresponds closely to Lewin's (1939) autocratic leadership style and that of McGregor's Theory X (1960) 'command and control paradigm', which we will return to in Chapter 7.

The country club leadership style demonstrates high concern for people but minimal concern for production. Leaders who score 1.9 on both dimensions are keen to foster a positive work environment even at the expense of output. In this style leaders assume that work will be carried out providing members feel secure, experience continuity (ie the maintenance of the status quo) and are content in their roles. Leaders in this role do not wish to 'rock the boat'; therefore they create an atmosphere that is reminiscent of a relaxed 'country club' environment.

At the opposite end of the spectrum lies the impoverished managerial style. Here managers display low concern for production and minimal concern for people. Ineffective leaders will score 1.1 on both dimensions. This approach to leadership relies on the goodwill of subordinates. Members who are exposed to this leadership style, however, more often than not feel uninspired. Often in such climates there is a feeling of desperation as individuals try to make sense of their working environment in their pursuit of survival.

The middle-of-the-road approach – with a score of 5.5 – represents medium concern for production and for people. This leadership style is not seen as very effective, as neither individual nor production needs are fully met. The middle-of-the-road approach is closely comparable to the laissez-faire style (Lewin, Lippitt and White, 1939), in which members are pretty much left to their own devices, and often in limbo. Ultimately, says industry leader Lewis Pullen, 'people do want to be led', and hence this approach is considered non-conducive.

Blake and Mouton identify 'team leader' as the most effective leadership style, with a score of 9.9. The managerial style exhibits high concern both for people and for tasks. Leaders who fall into this dimension understand the need for output and seek outcomes through collaboration. This approach is in alignment with Lewin's democratic and Katz, Maccoby and Morse's (1950) participative approach. While Blake and Mouton (1968) propose an ideal score of 9.9, some argue that this may not suit everyone; nor does it take into account the situational factors. The grid has also been criticized for its lack of cultural variation, offering an interesting alternative to the team leader preferred dimension and suggesting cultural dispositions could influence both the leader's style and subordinates' response. For example, in a study of cross-cultural attitudes Hofstede (1983) asserts that in individualistic societies more value is placed on individualism. People are more likely to look out for themselves and less likely to consider the needs of others. In Hofstede, Hofstede and Minkov's (2010) latest book, index scores are listed for 76 countries with a higher prevalence of social solidarity in East European, Latin, Asian and African countries than Germanic and English-speaking Western nations. Power Distance refers to the distribution of power and degree of inequality that exists among people. Nations with low Power Distance scores represent a balance in shared power. This means, organizational structures are likely to be flatter and more collaborative in practices. In contrast, in societies with high Power

Distance scores, distribution of power is unequal. In these circumstances, individuals will not dispute their given hierarchical status or ranking in the workplace. Leadership here is controlled and driven top-down, making the team leader dimension (in this situation) redundant since there is no need for team-based collaboration and therefore arguing against Blake and Mouton's preferred 9.9 score.

Despite the discrepancies surrounding culture, Blake and Mouton's grid still operates as a diagnostic and development tool in helping managers understand their behavioural patterns and functions. While Blake and Mouton maintain the ideal grid score is 9.9 because it embodies both interdependence and teamwork, what the grid fails to explain is situational variables. The latter will be introduced in the next section.

Contingency Theory

As previously highlighted, researchers in the field had begun to realize that there is no one 'best style' of leadership, that different situations demand different styles of leadership and that the theoretical models did not provide an adequate template for effective leadership. Researchers began to focus on a different variable: contingency. The idea behind contingency is that effective leaders will use a style of behaviour that fits the situation in which leadership is exercised. Interestingly, this belief was also shared by a number of interviewees, including Linda DeGrow, who 'truly believes that leadership is situational and the ability to adapt one's leadership style to fit situations is critically important'. Linda adds: 'When situations dictate, I will temporarily employ a command style of leadership to navigate through crisis. Ultimately, leaders must be able to assess the situation and the level of competence of their team, and quickly adapt to employ the style of leadership needed at the time.' Effectively this would demand a certain degree of emotional intelligence (EI) – see Chapter 7. Similarly, Louise Hill, former assistant general manager at Gaucho, affirms:

> I will sometimes be autocratic depending on the situation; if for
> example I'm new and things are not running well I will start out by
> making rules and regulations clear, setting clear goals and what we need

to achieve before taking any action against anyone who is not following standards. I will usually not keep this style for long. As I gain the respect of the team I can fall back to transformational leadership.

The first model to explore this concept was the Contingency Model set out by Fiedler (1967). Leader effectiveness is influenced by a number of variables, including his or her preferred behavioural style (see Figure 6.3) – relationship-oriented or task-oriented – and how favourable the leader's situation is (see Figure 6.4).

To assess the leaders' preferred orientation, Fiedler developed a measure coined the Least Preferred Coworker (LPC) scale. This scale identifies the person with whom the leader works least well. The leader is asked to rate (from 1 to 8) this person's characteristics on a 16-item scale. The results give the LPC score. Leaders scoring high LPC are considered person-orientated because they have the ability to be positive towards those they work least well with; in contrast, those scoring a low LPC are considered task-orientated. Leaders who score low LPC perceive

FIGURE 6.3   Leader's orientation

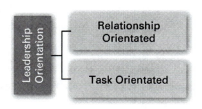

SOURCE: Adapted from Fiedler (1967).

FIGURE 6.4   Situational favourableness

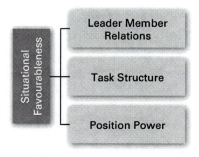

SOURCE: Adapted from Fiedler (1975).

their least preferred co-worker as negative and thus struggle to separate their personal views from members they connect least well to.

Fiedler's second measure is named situational favourableness: that is, the degree to which a situation enables the leader to exercise influence over his/her members. The degree of favourableness can vary from most, to moderately, to least favourable. Situational favourableness is dependent on three situational factors (see Figures 6.4 and 6.5).

The first factor, according to Fiedler, is leader–member relations that reflect the degree to which a leader is accepted and supported by his or her subordinates. This is dependent on the quality of the relationship between leaders and subordinates. Structural favourableness is the second factor and is determined by the structure of the task. This means that the more structured the task is (ie with more input and guidance regarding how a job is to be carried out), the more influence a leader will have over his/her members. This is particularly visible in command and control cultures, where members are constrained in how they must carry out their work. The third factor is position power, which concerns the degree of authority that leaders have to reward, punish or demote members. Effective leadership is thus optimal when leader–member relations are good, the task is highly structured and leaders have considerable position power. This combination places leaders in the most favourable position.

A number of criticisms have been directed at Fiedler's model. Some have argued against the validity aspect of the LPC scale, claiming there to be no direct evidence that high LPC leaders are necessarily person-orientated or that low LPC leaders are task-orientated. Similarly disputed is Fiedler's (1967) statement that effective leadership demands leaders to be flexible and adaptable so that they can act and manage different situations accordingly. The proposed solution, according to Fiedler (1967), is to tweak situations to fit the leader. However, this may not always be possible; for example, adjustment in the level of task structure may create unexpected or even greater problems for workers such as disturbance of working flow or role ambiguities. Notwithstanding this, the Contingency Model proved ground-breaking not only because it was the first to break away from the behavioural leadership movement, but precisely because it factored in situational aspects of organizational life.

Situational Leadership

The theoretical concept of situational leadership was introduced by Hersey and Blanchard in 1969 as the 'Life Cycle Theory of Leadership', and later renamed the Situational Leadership Theory (SLT). The theory proposes that the level of 'readiness' (discussed below) expressed by subordinates will determine which leadership style behaviour is the most suitable to use. In other words, the leader decides the degree of direction (ie task behaviour) and socio-emotional support (relationship behaviour) given the situation and level of maturity of his/her followers (see Table 6.5).

TABLE 6.5   Leadership style definitions

Task Behaviour is 'the extent to which the leader engages in spelling out the duties and responsibilities to an individual or group. This behaviour includes telling people what to do, how to do it, when to do it, where to do it, and who's to do it. In task behaviour the leader engages in one-way communication' (p 172).

Relationship Behaviour is a 'two-way communication process and its style is non-directional mainly because followers have the ability and motivation to take on responsibilities without the need for any supervision' (p 172).

SOURCE: Hersey and Blanchard (1988: 169–201).

Through sampling leader behaviour data from 459 employees working in a national retail chain, Hersey and Blanchard (1969) developed the Leader Effectiveness Adaptability Description (LEAD-Self) tool. The tool contains 12 possible leadership scenarios of the two behavioural style dimensions (ie task or relationship) that leaders can select from. The LEAD-Self scores provide feedback on leadership style, range and adaptability. The researchers characterized four leadership styles (S1–S4; see Table 6.6). Style range is the extent to which leaders are able to vary their leadership style. Style adaptability is the degree to which they can adjust their style according to the demands of a given situation.

The second factor in determining the best style of leadership described by the theory is readiness, which, as defined by Hersey and Blanchard

TABLE 6.6 Leadership styles (S1–S4)

Style (S1)	Above-average amounts of task behaviour Below-average amounts of relationship behaviour
Style (S2)	Above-average amounts of relationship behaviour Above-average amounts of task behaviour
Style (S3)	Above-average amounts of relationship behaviour Below-average amounts of task behaviour
Style (S4)	Below-average amounts of relationship behaviour Below-average amounts of task behaviour

SOURCE: Hersey and Blanchard (1988: 169–201).

(1988), refers to the person's readiness to carry out a particular task. Two additional components are ability and willingness, described as the degree to which an individual feels confident and committed to accomplish a task. The latter is also referred to as psychological maturity, as it assesses subordinates' motivation (intrinsic or extrinsic) and willingness to accept responsibility. In measuring subordinate readiness, two diagnostic instruments are used: the Manager's Rating Form and Self-Rating Form. The follower readiness continuum consists of four levels shown in Table 6.7.

TABLE 6.7 Follower Readiness (R1–R4)

R1	R2	R3	R4
Low readiness	Low to moderate readiness	Moderate to high readiness	High readiness
Unable and unwilling or insecure	Unable but willing or confident	Able but unwilling or insecure	Able and willing or confident

SOURCE: Hersey and Blanchard (1988: 169–201).

Therefore, the most appropriate leadership style is dependent on the readiness level of the followers. In facilitating this, Hersey and Blanchard propose four differing styles: Telling, Selling, Participating and Delegating (see Table 6.8).

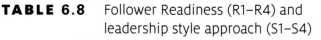

TABLE 6.8   Follower Readiness (R1–R4) and leadership style approach (S1–S4)

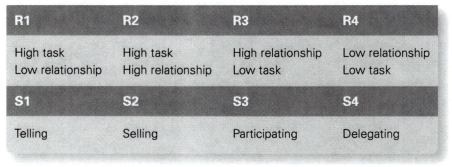

R1	R2	R3	R4
High task Low relationship	High task High relationship	High relationship Low task	Low relationship Low task
S1	**S2**	**S3**	**S4**
Telling	Selling	Participating	Delegating

SOURCE: Hersey and Blanchard (1988: 169–201).

Thus, readiness level (R1) and Telling style (S1) implies that leaders instruct subordinates on what to do, how to do it and when to do it. This is in contrast to the leadership style of Selling (S2), where subordinates show willingness but inability; here followers will function best under a leadership style that offers both guidance and support. The Participative style (S3) is particularly useful when subordinates find themselves at readiness level R3, where showing ability on the one hand yet appearing unwilling on the other. To facilitate this situation, the preferred style would encompass high levels of socio-emotional support but low amounts of leader direction. The optimum leadership style, according to Hersey and Blanchard, is that of Delegating (S4). At this level (R4), subordinates demonstrate ability, readiness and responsibility. Accordingly, leaders no longer need to be preoccupied with the task or the relationship. Subordinates in this position gain empowerment and begin to enjoy a high degree of autonomy. In bringing all the elements together, Hersey and Blanchard developed what is referred to as the model of situational leadership (Figure 6.5).

In summary, situational leadership is perceived as contextual and adapts to the readiness of followers (ie to carry out a particular task), suggesting the model provides scope for followers to develop and

FIGURE 6.5   Model of Situational Leadership

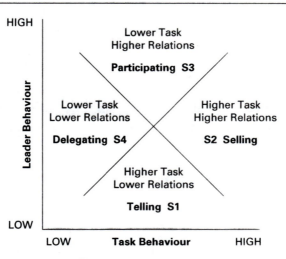

HIGH

Leader Behaviour

Lower Task
Higher Relations

Participating S3

Lower Task
Lower Relations

Delegating S4

Higher Task
Higher Relations

S2 Selling

Higher Task
Lower Relations

Telling S1

LOW

LOW   **Task Behaviour**   HIGH

SOURCE: Adapted from Hersey and Blanchard (1988).

grow. In doing so, subordinates must be motivated in wanting to advance, while at the organizational level systems must be in place to support them. At the same time, the model assumes that all leaders have the innate ability to assess and engage or understand the needs of each subordinate. The model also neglects to address other determinant factors, including the leaders' experience, since research (eg Collins, 2001) has illustrated that leaders who have a strong successful professional background do appear more flexible and varied in their leadership approaches. Nonetheless, Hersey and Blanchard's model is still widely used in leadership development programmes due to its flexible appeal and monitoring facets, which give leaders the opportunity to adjust to followers' different situational demands. What does seem to remain a critical weakness, however, is the assumption that all leaders have the potential to adapt their style(s) of leadership to any situation, once again drawing the discussion back to nurture versus nature.

Leader–Member Exchange Model

The Leader–Member Exchange (LMX) Theory moved away from the Ohio and Michigan leadership idea that all subordinates are treated in the same way. The theory proposes that leaders engage in varying social exchanges (see Figure 6.6), though not all relations develop into fruitful ones. The Leader–Member Exchange Theory of Graen and Uhl-Bien (1995) stems from Dansereau, Graen and Haga, who in 1975 developed the construct of 'Vertical Dyad Linkage' (VDL). Similar to VDL, LMX centres on a dyad, namely the relationship between leader and subordinate. It is the nature of this relationship that will distinguish between members of the in-group and the out-group.

FIGURE 6.6   Leader–Member Exchange (LMX) model

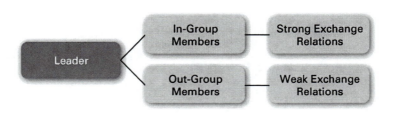

SOURCE: Adapted from Dansereau *et al* (1975).

Research in support of the LMX theory suggests that subordinates who share in-group status with leaders will experience greater job satisfaction (Graen and Uhl-Bien, 1995), higher motivation and better commitment towards the organization than might subordinates who feel left on the periphery. Leaders will grant greater autonomy, decision-making latitude and responsibility to in-group members. In exchange, in-group members receive greater recognition, support, promotion, monetary incentives and opportunities for their efforts (Hassan and Hatmaker, 2014). For members who find themselves on the periphery, the experience is very different, as noted by Samantha Faros: 'I often feel like an outsider and am now resigned to the fact that I will never be part of the inner circle. I guess it is what it is.'

In furthering our understanding of exchange relationships, the Social Exchange outlook stipulates that people carry out a cost–benefit analysis and, based on that, will determine the overall worth (or not) of a particular relationship (Blau, 1964). This psychological insight could explain the reasons and incentives related to why individuals enter into high-quality vertical dyads: after all, the rewards for in-group members are manifold. More about exchange theory in Chapter 7.

Doubts have been raised about the predictive power of the theory and its explanation of how in-groups are initially formed. More interesting perhaps is the question of whether subordinates can do anything to help secure their in-group status. It is suggested that members of in-groups are perhaps more savvy and better equipped with skills sets than members of the out-groups. Similarly, when followers and leaders meet for the first time, often both parties are unaware of each other's knowledge or experiences. This initial encounter is similar to the 'forming stage' of Tuckman and Jensen (see Chapter 3). In it the leader and the subordinate unknowingly follow a process (similar to the one discussed in Chapter 2) of causal sense-making. Individuals will tread with caution and simply carry out their roles (no more and no less than what is defined in the employment contract). Subordinates at this stage will be reluctant to go the extra mile. In the construction of any potential relationship, both parties will look from the start for cues (ie similarities, communication styles, non-verbal signals, personality traits). Leaders will decide if the 'chemistry' is right to disclose or begin to trust their followers and move on to the next relationship stage. For followers, their roles will be based on potential exchanges (see Chapter 7), motivation (ie intrinsic or extrinsic) and how well they 'play the game' in securing their place at the captain's table. If not, team members like Samantha are likely to be left on the sidelines.

Conclusion

The chapter has provided an overview of the main historical developments in relation to leadership theories and has provided insights into leadership qualities from leaders within industry. Leadership is a multi-faceted construct, with each theory providing a unique standpoint on the questions: 'What is leadership?' and 'What is considered effective leadership?' For trait theorists, leadership is trait specific yet with the understanding that not all leaders turn out to be good at leading. Situational theorists claim that different situations will demand different styles of leadership behaviour, though perhaps more important is the relationships leaders share with followers. While the current chapter provided a snapshot of how leadership is related to motivation and commitment, Chapter 7 will examine this in greater depth alongside the task and people skills that are quintessential to effective leadership. In Chapter 7 the leadership discussion will continue and a proposal for a more hands-on humanitarian approach to leadership will be made.

Motivation and engagement

07

The aim of this chapter is to understand what makes workers tick – what employees expect from employers and what employers expect from employees. The chapter will commence with the subject of motivation, with a particular focus on McGregor's (1960) Theory X Y accompanied by Maslow's (1954) Hierarchy of Needs Theory. The concept of the psychological contract (PC) is introduced and there is a discussion of the issues that can arise when this contract is breached. Perceptions of job satisfaction and possible generational differences regarding satisfaction and attitudinal differences regarding work through the eyes of industry leaders and graduates will be discussed. The chapter closes with a proposal for a more emotionally intelligent and humanitarian approach to working practices in an attempt to bring back the humane to organizational life. It is suggested that this approach to working practices will lead organizations to optimum and long-term success.

What motivates people?

Theory X Y

Based on the early works of Taylor (ie scientific management) on how to enhance the performance of workers, McGregor (1960) developed the model of Theory X Y. Previously termed management by objectives (Drucker, 1955), the concept evolved in the 1980s to performance management and served as a strategic framework in directing all parties (ie stakeholders, clients, shareholders) toward a mutually agreed goal (Armstrong, 2009). McGregor's first theory, Theory X, assumes that employees who are extrinsically driven are by default demotivated; unless incentives are monetary, workers will be unwilling to work. At the opposite end of the spectrum, managers hold the view that employees are self-motivated, take pride in doing a good job, show willingness and take on responsibility. The belief is that individuals hold intrinsic motivations and thus work because it is internally rewarding for the individual. This dimension is referred to as Theory Y. To assist managers in motivating their workers, McGregor devised two managerial styles to help accommodate workers on both continuums: authoritarian and participative (see Table 7.1).

TABLE 7.1   Theory X and Theory Y

Theory X Authoritarian	Theory Y Participative
Members avoid work	Members thrive when working
Members dislike work	Member enjoy work
Members resist supervision	Members accept direction
Members resist responsibility	Members exercise accountability
Members resist change	Members are open to change

SOURCE: Adapted from McGregor (1960).

If managers assume that their team dislikes work, they will exercise Theory X. This style presents an authoritarian leadership approach with one goal in mind: to get employees working. The main task for authoritarian managers here is to ensure job security, monetary incentives and appropriate working conditions. McGregor claims staff engagement and morale would automatically follow from this. Yet this is not necessarily the case: this approach does not take into consideration the complexities of human social relations such as individuals' need for engagement, belongingness and validation, or any other important aspects of working life. Similar components had also been found in the Hawthorne effect (Mayo, 1945) and among industry leaders. For example, Henrietta Lovell of the Rare Tea Company states: 'My staff will not get huge rewards like bankers but they still work equally hard because they know that they are contributing to something important.' Of similar opinion, Credit Sales, Evanita ten Napel of Mitsubishi UFJ Securities International claims: 'You need some reward as well; I think that's often thought of being the most important one, but I would call it the least important one of the list.' In contrast, Riccardo Genghini of Studio Notarile Genghini & Associati favours the renumeration package: 'I don't think there are many workers that would choose lower paid work. Pay and distance are the principal selection criteria for a job.' General Manager of Novotel Guy Lootens is adamant that 'if you pay peanuts you will get monkeys', arguing monetary incentives are pertinent. Lewis Pullen, former chief marketing officer of Qantas, simply acknowledges: 'Look, at the end of the day you're remunerating people and hopefully you're paying them what they should be paid for the job they're doing.'

Parallels have also been drawn between McGregor's Theory X and the transactional leadership style set out by Burns (1978), which is identified with the idea of exchange. In the words of Bennis and Nanus (1985: 218), 'management typically consists of a set of contractual exchanges, "you do this job for that reward"… a bunch of agreements or contracts.' Burns (1978) refers to this as management by exception. Under this rule, managers operate from a top-down and/or com- mand-and-control culture so as to sustain continuity until existing working practices no longer achieve their purposes (eg when workers no longer meet the required goals); then alternative work methods will be looked at. While transactional and authoritarian leadership styles may get the job done, they may not necessarily lead to genuine commitment or long-term job satisfaction.

This is a good moment to introduce the differences between management and leadership, since research into the differing roles claim the two concepts are distinct in their functioning. The most prominent difference lies in the degree of change: where management seeks to maintain the status quo, leadership seeks transformation. In close alignment with theorists (eg Burns, 1978; Drucker, 1992), the 32 industry leaders made clear distinctions between the two concepts (see Table 7.2).

TABLE 7.2   Management versus Leadership: qualitative data sets (N = 32)

Leadership		Management
Visionary	Role clarity	Short-term
Humility	Ideas	Organizational
Expectation	Autonomy	Systems
Inclusivity	Listening	Status quo
Goal clarity	Info sharing	Task-driven
Motivation	Planning	Driven by bottom line
Decision	Latitude	Power
Recognition	Resourceful	Regulations, policies
Strategy	Inspiration	Conformity
Rapport	Accountability	Resource allocation
Growth	Bottom-up	Persuasion
Mentoring	Visibility	Performance management
Empowering	Communication	Role allocation

When interviewees were asked what the difference is between leading and managing, organizational psychologist Ohad Maoz says: 'You can be a good manager by doing your duties and achieving your goals. Leadership is the ability to motivate people to go with you.' Allana Brindal at Wednesday adds: 'Managing is much more hands on; it is a functional role whereas leading is providing original thought and inspiration.' Jon Hall, Managing Director of PGIR, believes: 'Managing can be different in the sense that you are organizing people around systems to undertake different functions and processes within the organization.' He adds: 'People want to be involved in an organization that is showing them the vision and direction that they know they can contribute to.' In closing, Royal Marine Alan Litster notes: 'The thing that is instilled into us from the very start is to lead by example. I think you can be trained to be a very competent manager and I think it is quite easy to manage, but it is harder to lead, especially by example.' These interviews imply that while leadership focuses on envisioning and relationship building, management represent characteristics of control, processes and rationality – or as Drucker (2008: 14) sums up neatly: 'Management is doing things right; leadership is doing the right things.' Irrespective, both components are necessary and should not be separated from one another. Rather insightful heads will incorporate both dimensions where needed.

Psychological contract

Inherent to the relationship of work, the psychological contract (PC) helps to clarify the incentives workers can expect to receive for the time and effort they put in to the organization. Two types of contract present themselves. The relational psychological contract involves the long-term agreement by the employer to employee to provide job security in exchange for employees' organizational commitment. In contrast, the transactional psychological contract tends to be short-term in nature and driven by monetary incentives.

The PC, says Rousseau (1995: 9), is 'the individual beliefs, shaped by the organization, regarding terms of an exchange between individuals and their organization'. This is closely reminiscent of the theory of social exchange (Blau, 1964), in which the overall worth of a relationship is determined by its cost–benefit analysis. According to this view, individuals who envision greater potential benefits will be more likely to invest in a personal relationship. Therefore, if both parties benefit from a relationship, an exchange would be deemed worthwhile. While the PC is central to the employer–employee relationship (Maguire, 2002), it only works if the individual voluntarily consents to and accepts the promises agreed upon. These promises or agreements discussed by the parties may be about career progression, training, promotion opportunities or monetary incentives. Where previously unwritten mutual exchanges and expectations have been agreed, problems start to arise when either party experiences a shift in or breach of expectation. This will have a negative impact – so much so that it is termed a breach of contract and may trigger a range of emotions: discontent, demotivation, distrust, non-commitment and disloyalty (eg Coyle-Shapiro and Kessler, 2000).

Sometimes unmet promises (eg career progression, monetary incentives) and/or expectations (eg job roles) are the result of miscommunication earlier on in the selection phase. Such misunderstandings, says Michael Aldous of the LSE, 'can be reduced by simply asserting at the onset what can be expected'. This means having a thorough understanding of expectations. He adds:

> it is a difficult balance to manage but if you are open and you
> incentivize people with money and targets you need to be very clear
> about that in recruitment. Then you will hire people that are driven by
> those metrics; those people may very well not need a lot of pats on the
> back and hugs.

Motivational prompts – rightly or wrongly – will of course vary from one individual and/or sector to another. Chief Creative Director and Co-Founder of the Mill, Pat Joseph, highlights this difference in how motivation is driven in the creative/digital sector, saying: 'Here you reward people by giving them great work to work on; that is the primary reward, when they finish that job and show people (only their peers no one else). That is the thing that gets them going, it is respect from their peers really.'

According to Maslow's (1954) theory, humans progress through five motivational stages, each of which has hierarchical significance. The ultimate stage in the hierarchy is the need to self-actualize (ie to reach one's full potential), yet this is only achievable when individuals have serviced the preliminary needs. At the lowest hierarchical level, needs humans must first fulfil are the fundamental physiological necessities of human life (sleep, water, sex, breath, food, safety, home-ostasis and excretion), followed by the need for safety (health, well-being and finance). The third level involves the need for belong-ingness, where intimacy, building rapport and love form an important part of human life. This in turn leads to esteem (self-esteem and esteem from others). In the context of working life this would involve validation from peers, leaders and employers. Maslow's ideas imply that unless all these fundamental needs are in place, people cannot start to focus on other motivational incentives in life.

Unmet promises associated with the psychological contract may be the result of external influences. For example, changes in financial markets may force organizational restructuring or the need for down-sizing, or so workers are told. On occasions restructures require adjustments of job roles. In the worse scenarios, job descriptions are rewritten and workers (in some cases) must re-apply for their jobs. The employee – who has (let's say) held the role for 20 years – is suddenly asked to prove his or her worthiness. New job descriptions are thus tweaked or further tasks and/or roles are added. While this may not necessarily be a bad practice, providing changes are made with good intent and in negotiation with the jobholder, in some instances adjustments may prove disadvantageous. For example, when changes in role, previously unknown to the jobholder, require new sets of competencies, thus forcing the jobholder to downgrade if he or she no longer meets the new job role criteria. In some instances, this can even lead to job loss. While this employment practice is not illegal, it is alarming that it can allow employers to 'remove and/or push aside' workers at any time. It seems no contract will save them. Perhaps this could explain why University Reader Samantha Faros says that 'Most academics feel dispensable.'

Time to tune in

It seems, not much has changed since the findings presented by industrial psychologist Elton Mayo, who shared similar ideas (ie the importance of social relations, engagement, employees' contribution) to Henrietta Lovell, who argues: 'It is important to treat people as "more than just a cog in a machine". It is not just the tea itself or the margins I make or the profit I make.' With the current focus on results-driven trends, alongside stringent controls (procedures, policies and regulations, compliance, reputational risks), changes in global economies and organizations forced to downsize, it is no wonder employers and employees are feeling the strain. For some, including Dave Coplin, Chief Envisioning Officer of Microsoft:

> This ongoing push is proving counterproductive – so much so, that productivity has to some extent become a problem in itself. Lots of people I know spend their days just answering e-mails; they are not doing any work in the broader sense, and they are certainly not using the creativity that they have.

Managing Director of Hakkasan, Didier Souillat explains: 'if we think that we are going to be making the business more successful by making sure we squeeze every inch out of people on small things, that it will not work, so this is very short-term.' As to the reasons why some organizations are primarily focused on the short term, Didier explains it is:

> Because [an organization] needs to develop fast and there needs to be a return, the focus is short-term for the moment across sectors. There is no trust in the future for the moment, so it is short-term – you borrow the money to invest but you need a return quickly because you do not have the trust.

While Didier emphasizes that this does not apply to his business, his point reflects the current results-driven cultures of organizational life. Samantha Faros describes the short-term nature of her work culture, saying: 'It's like businesses want everything now, they don't understand the importance of longevity. Even the students don't seem to think long term. But for something to flourish you have to nurture it; give it time to grow.' This was echoed by Hugo Chapman of the British Museum who is also of the opinion that a short-term vision is not ideal:

> I think it is much better to have longer-term strategic vision. I mean, in my world you have to look a long way ahead to plan an exhibition. There are those others in my organization who find it difficult to think two years ahead; I have to think four or five years ahead.

At the same time, short-term goals may be pertinent due to the nature or context of the given business. In either case, perhaps the time has come to challenge the status quo, arguing the case that people are more than just cogs in a machine. As Henrietta Lovell explains, sometimes organizations 'lose sight of the employees while concentrating too much on the company as a whole... thinking what is best for the company, and regarding the company as something other than the people who work in it'. This raises the question of whether somehow we have regressed back to a variant of Taylorism where the focus is on results and the needs of the employee are neglected. If true, then this demands our attention as there is a cost not only to the individual employees but also to the effectiveness of the organization. For the individual this neglect can lead to discontent, demotivation, stress, non-commitment and disloyalty, and at the organizational level this can lead to absenteeism, turnover and financial consequences.

Successful organizations in contrast understand that their biggest asset is their people. This means, echoes Resort Manager Borja Manchado: 'It is important that you give priority to your people because it's all about the people.' A sentiment echoed by Alan Litster who re-affirms: 'Our business is our workers.'

This thinking demands a particular leadership style. With this in mind, we can build upon the emotional intelligence ideas of Goleman (1996) and the humanistic appproach. A new leadership dimension can be derived from qualitative interview data analyses with a greater focus on organizational humanity. The emotionally intelligent leader is said to meet the needs and values of both workers and key organizational (and non-organizational) players (ie management, shareholders, stakeholders, clients) in creating a positive working environment. The remainder of this chapter will thus describe the building blocks that address self-awareness and awareness of others' needs which are fundamental to effective leadership and how this links to job satisfaction and more successful organizations.

The emotionally intelligent leader

Leadership remains a multi-faceted construct, with each theory providing a unique viewpoint on the questions of what leadership is, and what makes good leaders. While a plethora of attempts have been made to provide a definitive answer to these questions, the general view is that successful leadership is a combination of both people and task-orientated practices. These conclusions are not new, yet what did interestingly materialize from the interview data analysis presented in this book is that strong leadership requires effective communication (as outlined in previous chapters) and a specific set of behaviours. The following section seeks to unpack these attributes with a focus on the quality of the human interaction. The three distinct dimensions include:

- **Self**: distinguishes the leader from non-EI leaders in that EI leaders show humility and through this attribute have the ability to self-reflect on their working practices and relationships with others.

- **Significant others**: This is about the ways in which leaders ought to behave with significant others. The idea is that EI leaders exhibit kindness and enjoy sharing success with others (eg members of the team).

- **Purpose**: This was developed from responses to the question: what is expected of EI leaders? EI leaders will not only be equipped with the 'humane' qualities that they exhibit to others in the organization, but also be clear about how to communicate the organizations' vision to their teams.

Let us begin with brief discussions of the first dimension: Self and its accompanied sub-themes of Humility and Self-reflection.

Self: Humility, Self-reflection

Linda DeGrow, former general manager of North American Operations at Voith Industrial Services, provides a good synopsis of what humanistic leadership could look like: 'A leader must demonstrate the values and ethics of the organization consistently and authentically, because he/she truly believes in them.' Authenticity has been described by Harter (2002: 382) as a person acting 'in accord with the true self, expressing oneself in ways that are consistent with inner thoughts and feelings'. Ideally, EI leaders are grounded and true to themselves.

This means they don't fake their leadership, but rather are driven by morality; this means leaders exhibit behaviour in sync with their values and belief systems (Sparrowe, 2005). This encourages employees to follow their lead, as Linda DeGrow describes: 'Being authentic, being true to my and the company's values on a consistent basis, means my team knows what to expect from me, in terms of behaviours and responses.' This means, emphasizes Pat Joseph, it is fundamental to

> treat people as you would want to be treated, so they will be as you want them to be. If you treat them badly for a while they will do what you want them to do because they will do it out of fear, but they will not do more than you want them to do and they will not do better.

What Linda and Pat ultimately emphasis is that behaviour effectively drives the behaviour of others. Also typical of EI leadership is the sense of humility, though as Jon Hall admits:

> [It] is difficult to put into words. You can just see it in a person: they are people who stand out in a crowd, are referred to all the time, tend to get on with everyone, have their own views and seldom get caught in a clique. They are not necessarily the nosiest or loudest person, [but] people are attracted to them and tend to group physically and emotionally around them; peers look up to them.

Similarly, adds Samantha Faros, 'true leaders who show humility yet remain strong and have the capacity to draw people towards them.' Moreover, Drucker (1992: 14) describes: 'Leaders who work most effectively... never say "I". And that's not because they have trained themselves not to say "I". They don't think "I". They think "team". They understand their job to be to make the team function.' A view Evanita ten Napel agrees with: 'I can see very well what is happening and what people are doing. I can give very good advice and help people to see things in a different light.' This implies that EI leaders are not ego-driven; rather they are focused more on others. Perhaps it is this attribute that makes them different from other leadership figures. In summary, and in setting the scene for the next leader dimension – self-awareness – Linda DeGrow affirms that a good leader is someone 'with humility – who will admit mistakes and admit what they don't know'.

In becoming a better leader, Zaleznik (1977) claims that leaders who are self-aware – defined here as 'the development of an awareness of the self and one's own view of the world' (Moon, 2003: 82) – will have a desire to self-improve and do so by drawing upon others for feedback. This idea is reminiscent of Maslow's (1954) concept of self-actualization, wherein individuals are innately driven to better themselves but not out of self-centredness; rather, it provides a positive platform that permits individuals to work within themselves. EI leaders will be keen to set this example. Moreover, says Chris Butt, CEO of Cognisess: 'If you can self-reflect and understand strengths and weaknesses, build a supportive team around you, that will enable you to take things forward.' Thus the ability to self-reflect – described by Boyd and Fales (1983: 100), as 'internally examining and exploring an issue of impact triggered by experience, which creates and clarifies meaning in terms of self, and which results in a changed conceptual perspective' – is considered the second humanistic leader dimension that emerged from the qualitative data set. Chris Butt goes on to say: 'If there is one characteristic of being a good leader, it is your ability to reflect and then act on that reflection. If you are doing self-reflection over time... you are able to make decisions based on your informed knowledge.' Likewise, Linda DeGrow affirms: 'Good leaders willing to seek feedback about their leadership abilities and continuously work at being a better leader.' Practising self-reflection can lead to change. According to Mezirow (1992), there are three types of transformational practices. Content reflection focuses on the content or description of a particular problem, while process reflection focuses on the strategies used in solving the problem and premise reflection questions the assumptions and beliefs that frame the problem.

Not all reflective practice leads to change though. One reason explains Chris Butt: 'It is too easy for us to ignore our inner conversations, acting on that is too difficult.' Two sets of cognition are said to influence the transformational process. The first is self-efficacy: that is, one's self-belief and capacity to perform a specific task (Locke and Latham, 2004). Self-efficacy thus regulates behaviour and motivation. This also links in to the notion of locus of control, which is the degree to which individuals feel in control (or not) of the influences and circumstances that drive their behaviour. The second cognitive influence is goal orientation (Dweck and Leggett, 1988), which is split either into performance or learning-orientated behaviour. Performance-goal-orientated individuals are more focused on the end result, do not like to fail, and focus on the consequences of their poor performance, especially the disapproval of others. They want to be positively evaluated by others. In contrast learning-goal-orientated individuals are not concerned about what others think. Rather they are keen to learn new skills and master new situations. People who exhibit learning-goal-orientated tendencies are more likely to undergo conceptual change as they can attribute failure or mistakes to themselves rather than blame external factors. This means reflecting upon their choice of strategy or decision-making processes so as to improve them. It is precisely this awareness, suggests Chris Butt, that distinguishes poor from, 'good leadership, which is about understanding your own limits'. So much so, echoes Didier Souillat, that good leaders create 'an association of talents and leadership, in this case making sure you have got enough talent around you that complements you'. EI leaders are distinguishable because they possess high self-efficacy and internal locus of control, alongside a strong sense of self. This makes them more open and receptive to learning and confident enough to reflect upon past events, because they know that they will be in a position to do better next time.

Significant others: kindness, sharing success

EI leaders will be mindful and kind in their relations with significant others. For Henrietta Lovell, the concept of kindness – something much undervalued in organizational life – appears to be second nature. She emphasizes: 'It is essential to Rare Tea to think about our customers and our suppliers and the people who work with in the business with kindness and [ensure] that they are always looked after as best we can.' Samantha Faros agrees with this view: 'It doesn't cost anything to show kindness. If people were kinder to one another both in and outside work, I think the world would be a better place.' It is difficult to ascertain why kindness is not more embedded in our working cultures. Perhaps the concept is misunderstood, as Alan Litster explains: 'A lot of people make the mistake that they think they should be a friend of the person that they are leading. This is not what the led want at all; they want someone that they can trust and that is not necessarily someone that is who is their best friend.' Similar misinterpretations may be held in relation to kindness, for example that kind leaders are perceived as weaker or that kindness is not considered an attribute at all compared to the usual traits (eg authoritarian, dominant, strong, see Chapter 6) that leadership is associated with. All in all, kindness is and ought to be included in the listing of leader attributes, since most of us will be receptive to it.

The Action-centred Leadership Model prescribed by Adair (1973) recommends leaders praise their team members when they do well. Likewise, EI leaders recognize that sharing success is important. Lewis Pullen affirms: 'Sharing [it] around can help build a very powerful team.' It is this insight that takes the EI leader dimension to a different level, as Lewis Pullen goes on to say: 'Leadership is about not taking all the glory.' Rather, explains Roland Esnis at IBM, it is about: 'sharing ownership among team members'. This too is affirmed by Professor of Surgery and former head of department at University Hospital of Caen Guy Samama, who says 'It gives your team the opportunity to also share the limelight, the success, not only you!' Likewise, Linda DeGrow comments: 'I encouraged all members of my team to share successes and failures during our quarterly business meetings.'

What these findings further reveal is that acknowledgement is likely to strengthen team spirit and camaraderie. Chris Butt explains: 'People are looking for validation in their job; I think that is number one.' This simple gesture, according to Guy Kendall 'is very important. You are the leader, managing your team, you praise them when they do a good job and you tell them.' Similarly Allana Brindal understands the importance of reinforcement, describing her agency as:

> ... pretty savvy. They know that people like positive reinforcement. If people are going to be working back till 9 pm on a consistent basis then they've got to be happy, that they're going to get rewarded. People work really long hours, like sometimes a 12-hour day.

Guy Kendall goes a step further by suggesting: 'I believe in thanking people for their efforts and celebrating individual and group success.' Louise Hill, formerly of Gaucho, agrees employees should be acknowledged and 'thanked for their hard work'. Yet this practice must be done with integrity, Pat Joseph affirms: 'I praise people when I think praise is due. I would not praise when I do not think it is not due because people will not trust you as they will think they do not deserve it.' Pat goes on to say: 'The whole point of work is people need to smile, they need to feel good about it, they need to feel proud of who they are working for and they need like the environment that they are working in and they need to get job satisfaction out of it.'

The message here is that when leaders share successes by recognizing peoples' hard work, this sets a positive tone. If organizational cultures are founded upon making employees feel valued, it is likely members will instinctively want to participate or be willing to go the extra mile, knowing that at the end they have added value or made some contribution that is recognized. This gives people job satisfaction and may even diminish the problem of social loafing (see Chapter 4).

Purpose: vision, communication

Humanistic leaders have purpose and understand what is expected of them, and ultimately how they and their team fit into the overall vision of the organization. Kirkpatrick and Locke's (1991: 37) traditionalist view of vision describes it as the 'main technique that effective leaders use to inspire followers to perform exceptionally well'. The technique is founded on influence. Yet influence comes about in different ways. For EI leaders, influence is integral and is orchestrated through engagement and communication with stakeholders. Maike van der Hooghen of the Dutch MOD affirms that this involves maintaining 'personal contact with the employees and [having them] explain their thinking process... It enables them to make decisions on their own, within the vision and goals as set out by the management. So you develop trust.' The organizational vision is most effectively developed when it is collectively created and suffices for all parties (ie management, stakeholders, employees). This is further achieved through the 'process of personal identification, whereby the individual's belief about a person [a leader] becomes self-referential or self-defining' (Avolio *et al*, 2004: 806). This process, explain Kark and Shamir (2002), helps move people toward a vision, as leaders become familiarized with their members' values and belief systems. It is suggested that such connecting practice will increase members' receptiveness and willingness to move in the same direction as their leaders – providing, says Henrietta Lovell, employees 'expect a vision for the company and their role within it'. EI leaders want to ensure their members are on board. In doing so, echoes Lewis Pullen, the 'actual strategic process needs to be quite inclusive, and if you have buy-in to that then people think they are part of the team.' Key to this process is communication. Communicating with clarity is thus crucial, as Maike van der Hooghen comments: 'It is vital to maintain an open and transparent channel of communication and to explain why certain decisions are made or have to be made. For example, to make employees understand why short-term decisions and goals – which may be difficult to understand – are important within the long-term vision.' Or as Simon Lloyd notes: 'being able to communicate, being able to take complex and difficult issues and turn them into simple issues'. For Riccardo Genghini, leadership involves the ability to 'communicate and guide, particularly in hardship following defeat or in preparing for victory, to those who are led'. Thus, EI leaders will opt for transparency and openness. First off they listen and absorb what is being said to them, reflect, and thereafter find a suitable way to transfer this message, knowledge or information to their teams.

According to Linda DeGrow: 'Fostering an environment of openness and candour helps to build trust among its workforce.' This idea of openness allows members to be honest in their communication with one another. Maike van der Hooghen explains: 'At work I try to be open to [other staff's] views, listen and ask as well as give feedback, in order to create mutual understandings.' Likewise, at the LSE, Michael Aldous adds:

> There is a lot of communication that comes from the Directorate asking for input throughout the organization. They are interested in understanding what you think about LSE, where you think it should go, what is important, how processes should be managed. So I think they have been pretty open, they are trying to foster a collegiate spirit.

This approach is well understood by the scientific director of the Mathematical Institute of Leiden University, Peter Stevenhagen, who explains that communication 'is really important and I do like a direct way of communicating with people, without many layers in between. For an institute like ours, which is small, this seems to be a successful strategy, as it enables me to let people do what they're good at, without imposing uniform rules.' Ex-rugby player, Jon Hall agrees the direct approach is best, one that instils: 'complete honesty, not being frightened to speak our minds is good leadership practice and improves working relationships within the work team environment'. But John also recognizes that: 'people spend a lot of time walking on eggshells in the workplace', suggesting that perhaps we are not as open as we would like to be.

Either way, clearly defined communication channels will reduce confusion. Industry leader Guy Lootens describes the importance of being 'very open-minded [and] direct in answers: is it a yes or a no? And if I can't give an answer, then I set a deadline for when I'll give them one. That is very important for people and they trust you. They then don't have to worry or think about it because they know they will have [an] answer.' If not, Michael Aldous describes: 'I think there [can be] a real lack of clarity, and it goes right up to the top, about what a firm actually does and what it stands for.' Communication and clarity thus go hand-in-hand, as Allana Brindal affirms:

> Clarity I think is the main thing. I think I'm pretty clear in my communication with clients and I'm very conscientious with attention to detail, documentation and all of the things... you have to produce in order to kind of, get a client to sign with you, I think I've got quite a good process for getting that down and for interpreting the client's requirements. It's completely transparent, and I make sure I re-assure them that I know their brand, and that the agency can handle all of their requirements as well, whether that be providing them with a creative brief or a scope-of-work document that outlines everything we're delivering.

In relation to this, Chapter 4 noted that planning, appointing roles and allocating resources helped members to focus on their tasks. In doing so, Adair suggests that the first function leaders must perform is ensuring members are clear on what needs to be done. This means (early in the planning stage) identifying individuals' expertise and experience pool, in a bid to match these to the roles and requirements of the task. EI leaders understand that individuals will be more motivated and committed to goals when roles are clearly stated to them and are realistic. If not, the latter can lead to role ambiguity or conflict (see Chapter 4). The idea is: the more open and transparent we are in our communication style, the more receptive people will be, and the less ambiguity members of the organization will feel.

Bringing back the humane

Key to EI leadership is the realization that unless organizations redirect their focus on the people, those at the forefront will be less committed and dedicated to the organization's cause. The three humanitarian expressions – as part of EI – that emerged from the qualitative data set include: making people feel valued, showing care and providing support. These are said to promote positive working cultures and motivation.

Making people feel valued

The first humanitarian theme linked to what motivates workers is about value. A study by the Institute of Leadership and Management (ILM) reported that of 1,001 workers interviewed, 16 per cent are prepared to resign from their job if they do not feel valued (CIPD, 2013). Resourcing and talent planning adviser Claire McCartney at the Chartered Institute of Personnel Development (CIPD) goes further: 'Now more than ever, employers need to focus on ensuring their line managers are equipped with excellent people management skills, so they can play their role in fostering open and transparent cultures where people feel they can make a valued contribution and get recognition for it' (CIPD, 2013: 2.). Chances are, says Linda DeGrow, that people who feel undervalued are likely to leave. Linda adds: 'In my opinion, feeling valued is the single most important aspect of our work. For me, when there was a time in my career that I did not feel valued, I knew it was time to find a new place to work.' In close alignment with the CIPD survey of 2013, Samantha Faros adds that though she is 'passionate about the teaching' and admits 'this keeps me going', she feels that 'outside the feedback of students, there is no real wider sense of belonging.'

Two other interviewees also highlighted the need to make people feel valued expression. Didier Souillat affirms: 'It is all about the people' and Borja Manchado explains that: 'We have a yearly employment opinion survey and to the survey question "I feel proud to work for the Four Seasons", obviously this is the most important score.' Borja adds that ultimately employees at his hotel are made to feel valued. This too is articulated by industry leader Henrietta Lovell, who emphasizes:

> Key to my business success is my people – my company is made up of the people who work for it. If I do not have that strong relationship with my farmers, my team and my customers, I am sure I would not have such a successful business. They are all part of my company and I want them to feel proud to be involved and committed.

Similarly, Evanita ten Napel says: 'My personal opinion is you have to feel valued and respected.' Employers need to begin to understand that it does not require much effort to make workers feel valued, but it brings with it an abundance of goodwill and satisfaction. Pat Joseph also shared this viewpoint: 'What is important is that they feel that they have produced something that they feel happy with.'

The concept of trust is deeply rooted in many aspects of organizational life and can play out in different forms – first being the trust that exists between the employer and their employees. Borja Manchado proudly shares that, at the Four Seasons Hotel, 'There is a lot of trust. We talk to people, you know, we have departmental meetings, we have staff parties, we do monthly recognition celebrations for employees and you can feel that.' Riccardo Genghini believes organizational trust is experienced when 'there isn't a gap between what one says and what one does; when human expectations are met; when one's behaviour is consistent and therefore predictable.' Yet a relatively recent (2011–2012) online survey found, alarmingly, that of 2,047 UK employees surveyed, the majority did not trust the leadership style of their organization. Senior managers in the public sector in particular were deemed by their staff to be less trustworthy than voluntary and private sector managers (CIPD Employee Outlook

Survey, 2013). Perhaps the views of some workers tie in with Didier Souillat's comment that: 'You have to earn that loyalty. Once you show loyalty this too will enhance greater trust.'

There can also be an issue of trust between managers and subordinates. This manifests itself in various forms, such as the degree of leverage (eg decision-making latitude, job control) workers receive. In close alignment with Karasek's Job Demand Control Model (see Chapter 5), Dave Coplin reiterates: 'I think it all comes down to control, mostly about how much control I have about what is going on. Regardless of your work or the skills that you have, you should be encouraged and welcomed to contribute to the outcome of the organization', even when working practices go wrong. Hugo Chapman, who draws upon the notion that while employers demonstrate trust by giving their employees responsibilities, employees in turn must have trust in the employer – whether trust in general or trust that their employers will be prepared to go above and beyond what is commonly seen as their duty. This is also recognized by Maike van der Hooghen, who says: 'It is important to back employees when one of their decisions or actions has gone wrong. You have to stand by your employees in order to develop trust.' Hugo Chapman affirms: 'I think they seek people who will trust them, give them responsibility, and if things go wrong they will stand by them and take the blame along with them and not just expose them and leave them... I would not leave them exposed. I will be there for them and shoulder the blame with them.' The assumption is that the greater the trust, the more secure subordinates will feel. Trust, according to Dirks and Ferrin (2002), will eventually lead to organizational buy-in as well as commitment (Butler, Cantrell and Flick, 1999) and for this reason, as highlighted earlier, employees will be willing to go the extra mile. Effectively a win–win situation for all – a concept that is well understood by a number of the interviewed industry leaders.

A third aspect is trust that exists among co-workers; according to Dave Coplin, of Microsoft:

We have seen [shortage of trust] play out in flexible working practices, so if I am not in the office, it is more likely that my colleagues are going to think that I am skiving rather than they would of my boss. The people who work outside of the office feel so guilty that their colleagues might be thinking this about them that they try to overcompensate; they send more e-mails, make more phone calls, try to be more visible and say "I am not here, but look I am working." That is a detrimental effect of trust issues.

Several interviewees discussed different ways to build trust and what trust implied, beginning with Borja Manchado: 'It's very important that you make yourself visible, you make yourself available. My door is always open.' Along similar lines, Didier Souillat explains it is important to 'work intelligently [and] be there – people need to see you and people need to know you are there; you need to respond. People need to know you are there and the door is open, they can always walk in.' For Linda DeGrow trust means 'doing what I say I'm going to do. I do not operate with hidden agendas. People trust me as a result of my actions and behaviours, which they observe over time.' After all, Linda adds: 'Gaining and keeping the trust of my team and my customers is what provides a competitive advantage.' When trust is breached however, we find ourselves in uncertain territory, as evidenced in university reader Samantha Faros' comment: 'Trust is important and I think it is instrumental in maintaining workable relationships. Yet when the trust has gone, it is difficult to regain it.' In conserving the trust, stipulates Didier Souillat, it is critical to 'practise what you preach'. People in the group will never understand if someone at the top is not doing what he preaches. That will show the trust is broken very quickly.' This too is echoed by Michael Aldous:

> If top management doesn't believe in its mission, then it is difficult to care, and if you personally do not care it is very difficult to transmit positivity to other people. In the companies that have clarity and do that well, the top people care, and if the top care that will go all the way down the chain.

Incidentally, this brings us to the second humanistic expression said to assist motivation.

Showing care

Let's turn to the question: what do employees expect from employers? The data analyses (N = 32) revealed a secondary humanitarian insight: show care. This was raised by Didier Souillat, who highlights: 'If you take care of the people they will take care of you, it is as simple as that.' Flight dispatcher Robert de Vos, of KLM, explains the concept of loyalty as 'being taken care of – that's really important, and in return you work hard for your employer, of course'. Of a similar opinion is Ohad Maoz, who adds: 'Treat your workers in a fair and honest way and take care of them, and you will get the results you want.' Furthermore, says Allana Brindal, it is the little things that count

> like giving people nice laptops, like MacBooks and like, being able to, you know, unlimited Spotify account so we're encouraged to put on music throughout the day... yeah we play music at work, which is really important; it reduces the stress levels. They put fruit bowls around, every Friday they put on a really nice breakfast so everyone's encouraged to sit down together from all the agencies and talk about the projects over breakfast and it makes everyone come in by nine on a Friday which is good. They've got a 'Ride To Work' scheme, there's nice little perks – they have a massage scheme as well so you can get £15 massage or something, little things like that.

Reasons as to why some organizations simply fail to care are suggested by Louise Hill, who says: 'I don't think all employers care about their employees' needs but simply want bodies that will get the job done; some employers want you to give your whole life to their business as if it is your own.' Shai Greenberg expresses a similar point: 'I think in an ideal world you would like the employees to think the business is their own and treat it like that. It is hard to get people thinking like that and to treat it as their own.' While Chris Butt simply articulates: 'Some people are more passionate about people and some people are not. We always feel that people should be of an equal standard but humans are incredibly complex, driven by lots of different things. It is just down to the complex nature of who we are as humans.'

Providing support

The third humanitarian theme linked to what motivates workers that emerged from the qualitative data analysis is providing support – at task, development and personal level. To begin, research links have been made between task-related support and motivation. Amabile and Kramer (2010) did a qualitative analysis of nearly 12,000 diary entries and found that motivation and emotions were strongly correlated with workers' ability to make progress. The study showed that workers' having the necessary resources and aids to progress with their work – or, as Amabile and Kramer define it, 'make headway' – is considered a strong motivational component of performance. The study thus concluded that workers who are given sufficient control to 'make headway' and who receive support when necessary display the highest motivation levels. In particular, the emphasis on support in difficult times is also captured by Roland Esnis who says: 'Employees look for support to remove roadblocks, seek collaboration in decision-making and want to be protected against hierarchical pressures.' This is also recognized by Louise Hill, who adds: 'Employees should be able to expect support, the resources to do the job they are being asked to achieve, respect as an individual, understanding.' Former Middle East Correspondent, Joris Luyendijk, believes:

> [Trust] is a consequence of [recognition]. Once you recognize the legitimate demands and expectations on the part of your employee, this will come across as respect... It makes a huge difference if the top is seen to be going out of its way to be supportive. Generally I'd say some employers foster a nurturing culture from the top all the way down.

Parallels are found between Amabile and Kramer (2010) and Karasek's (1979) JDC Model (see Chapter 5), in which control and support systems are reported as crucial components of working life. When workers feel disabled or do not receive support, this will affect their moods and motivation levels and will lead to dissatisfaction. Thus, Amabile and Kramer (2010) suggest that those who regulate resources and have the power to provide support should ensure that systems are in place to respond to workers' needs. Guy Lootens adds: '[Ultimately] employees want honesty and they want employers to be involved with their problems, have solutions; they want employers to be involved with their daily work. I could work 24 hours behind my computer and staff will not see me. Staff need to see that I am around.' Along similar lines, Maike van der Hooghen affirms that employees look for 'loyalty, an open ear, problem-solving (so that people can do their work) and feedback'. Good leaders will monitor output and progress, and provide support accordingly.

Thus the support dimension covers a wide range of activities as well as development opportunities, as a number of industry leaders stipulate. First up, Allana Brindal says:

> You people to go away feeling good. I think it's really nice to give
> people positive reinforcement and they walk away from it feeling good
> You can sit there and talk about any objectives that have been set and
> whether they feel they are tackling those objectives or if they feel they
> need new ones set, because they want a promotion or... so they have a
> say as well, so it's a forum to, kind of, talk about what they're wanting
> from their career, how they want to get there, any additional kind of
> training or education they feel like they need.

Alan Litster reiterates: 'It is about them: their career, their aspirations, what they want to do, have they got any problems, and it's known as a sort of 'one-on-one' process where I make myself accessible. They don't need to put their hand up and ask to speak to you: you go to them.'

Support is also expressed at personal level, by leaders showing interest in their employee's well-being – as Simon Lloyd of Santander explains, it is vital to 'emotionally engage with people'. Evidence of strong engagement practices was provided by the industry leaders interviewed for this book. Maike van der Hooghen explains: 'On a personal level, you can show an interest in them rather than communicate about work all the time. There has to be space to release the pressure now and then, like an informal chat for instance about their holiday destinations.' Lewis Pullen of Qantas declares: 'I always make a point when I fly to sit down with the crew and say "Look, I head up marketing" and if there is any time during the flight the crew want to get a bit of an update of what is going on, I'm happy to talk about it.' Similarly, Didier Souillat explains: 'I am fairly open. I know the people there and they know me. I know their names, I know where they work. I say, "Hi, how you doing today? Everything good? How are you feeling?' Guy Lootens also makes the time to get to know his staff: 'Yes, I speak to everybody. I know about my staff and I ask about their family. If I know that they have problems I try to give some signals.' Allana Brindal says: 'Just having little chats and actually being interested in people's personal lives as well. You do need to care about the whole picture, otherwise you don't know what's going on – like someone could come to work really stressed out and there might be a reason but you don't know.' Similarly, Jon Hall affirms: 'I like to put myself in the position of the employee and I would want to be dealing with a manager who is caring and understanding. I think this builds respect, honesty and understanding.' Henrietta Lovell says: 'Employers must show care to workers as opposed to cogs in a machine.'

The simple exercise of 'getting to know your workers' will improve relations. One department that plays a vital role in this arena is Human Resources. Perhaps here too it is time to press the pause button and to review what HR professionals are actually doing in trying to get to know their work force. Evidence of good HR practice was clearly identified by Human Resource Director Isabelle Minneci, who notes that: 'People are at the core of the strategy and are instrumental to the success and the growth of the company. Therefore staff development and growth is paramount to the way we do Human Resources at L'Oréal.' This hands-on approach is not necessarily sector-wide, as London-based academic Samantha Faros laments: 'I would not go to HR for any problem; I would rather speak to a colleague.' While this may not ring true for all HR departments, the point is that the whole idea behind the human relations legacy (see Chapter 1) is about looking after workers. With this in mind, it would be interesting to further document the relationships between employees and their HR departments, as well as to research what other practices they adopt in getting to know their workforce.

Attitudes to work

Surveys such as the CIPD's 2013 study show differing levels of employee engagement. Scores vary between sectors, with voluntary sector workers the most engaged, at 51 per cent, compared with the public sector at 37 per cent and private sector workers at 36 per cent (CIPD, 2013). Disengagement will influence individuals' attitudes towards work, which in turn will impact their degree of job satisfaction.

In one of a series of questions compiled by the Autumn Employee Outlook survey (CIPD, 2013), figures reveal an overall job satisfaction score of +40. The most satisfied workers were those in the voluntary sector, at +54, compared with public sector workers, at +41, and the private sector showing even lower scores at +39. Suggestions are that low levels of job satisfaction are perhaps related to workers feeling uncertain about their job security. This was particularly evident for public sector workers, who expressed greater concern over potential job losses than voluntary sector and private sector jobholders (Wilmott, 2011). Since 2011, the public sector has seen job losses of 270,000 (ONS, 2012b) and, affirms Ashman (2013), two-thirds of the reduction deemed necessary by the current government is still outstanding. The forecast is for the reduction in government general employment (GGE) to continue to spiral by a further 730,000 between 2011 and 2017 (OBR, 2012). In the private sector, however, 1.7 million jobs have been created since 2010 (ONS, 2013). The explanations being sought as to why workers feel dissatisfied and/or disengaged tap perhaps into uncertainties surrounding job security. The Employee Outlook Autumn Survey (2013) also detected interesting findings specific to age: older employees (55+ years) felt greater job satisfaction than the group of 18- to 24-year-olds.

Thus, to the question: do you notice generational differences (Gen X: born 1961–1981; Gen Y: born 1982–2000) in working attitudes? Of the 32 interviewees, surprisingly, only a handful (N = 9) believed there were noticeable differences. The first to share his view was Chris Butt: 'I am sure there are differences; no doubt the generation which is growing up with the internet as a standard tool compared to the previous generation has a different world view about how quickly things can be done.' Roland Esnis is also of the opinion that generational differences exist, affirming: 'X people have obviously not the same expectations as Y. Y have a lower appetite for management and fewer expectations from work.' Ward Edmonds, manager at TrateMedia JLT, agrees: 'Yes, Generation Y are less likely to be concerned by constant change, are used to multi-skilling and are used to shifting attention from one thing to another much more quickly.' There is a widespread view that Gen Y are 'the Entitlement Generation' (Twenge, 2007) or, in Didier Souillat's words, 'are not very hungry –

they think everything is due to them but they do not want to give back to society.'

From a completely different angle, Shai Greenberg at Gielly Green believes the issue is not generational; rather 'It is personality: some people are more ambitious than others. Some would push for more and [they are] the sort of people I want to work with, who would attract me to employ them.' Louise Hill muses: 'I am not sure… I notice some of the younger ones not taking it very seriously but then… [that is] probably the way I was at that age, so I'd have to say I don't notice too much difference.' Lewis Pullen philosophically adds:

I don't actually think it's generational, I just think it's the nature of the beast… [they] are really young and you want them to have the energy and the confidence and self-belief and actually not to be tainted by other things… you want to kind of let them be free within the organization to question and create change and innovate… you do not want to suppress that.

Similarly, Jon Hall explains:

We have a lot of young people in the office. They are what I would describe as modern-day employees who embrace new technology; the older employees have higher working standards, time keeping and so on, but they do not share the same technical skill sets… I don't find this difficult to manage [but] I do notice different points of view from older members of staff that sometimes prove challenging.

Equally unconvinced is Peter Stevenhagen, who admits: 'I'm not sure it's much beyond what you typically know. I mean people in their 20s can be of a different nature from people in their 60s.'

The above findings reveal a differing perception that generational differences do exist and are likely to impact working attitudes – rightly or wrongly. For example, compared to Gen Xers, Gen Y are seen to be more versatile; they 'easily incorporate the values of openness, collaboration, and innovation', according to L'Oréal's human resources director, Isabelle Minneci. Maike van der Hooghen observes that Millennials (ie Gen Y) are mostly branded as having 'little patience and understanding for working practices'. Equally, affirms Linda DeGrow: 'They seem to be more adaptable to changing environments, are quite efficient, and want explanations for what and why things are.' Yet, she adds: 'this explanation-seeking can create conflict when their "need-to-know" is misunderstood as resistance.' However, if appropriately nurtured, generations can learn to work in tandem as well as appreciate one another's expertise and point of views, as Isabelle Minnecci explains: 'Having both generations working together actually enriches the dynamic of an organization providing you find the best ways to play on each generation's strengths.' You need the right measures are in place to facilitate this process. For instance, curriculum educators who design management, leadership and MBA degree courses could embed best practice where graduates are taught how to work side-by-side with different types of people. Innovative practices have been implemented, for example, at L'Oréal, where differing generations act as each other's mentors. Isabelle Minneci describes this process: 'In Digital, we have developed a reverse mentoring programme whereby the younger generation teaches the older generation the basic principles of Digital. This [has proven] to be very efficient and creates further bonding and connections between generations.' An humanitarian approach could further bridge this gap by guiding people toward better attitudes and working practices. As Maike van der Hooghen, affirms 'I would rather have someone without the correct academic background, but with a positive and constructive work attitude.' The essential message is that poor work ethics, regardless of generation type, will ultimately affect employability.

Closing comments

Understanding how to motivate a workforce is key to the future of successful organizations. Many of us spend a large part of our lives in the workplace, and the evidence presented suggests that happy workers who feel respected and valued in their jobs are more productive. It is hoped that the book has provided a better under-standing of the theory by which organizational culture can be enhanced: for example, how behaviours and attitudes create a working culture which impacts directly upon innovation and ultimately performance, and the insight that people matter, regardless of their place in the hierarchy or how small or complex the organization. This poses an interesting question as to where we go from here in the world of work. One suggestion is that we incorporate the humanitarian expressions of value, care and support, to help redirect our focus back onto the people. Thus, readers are asked to press their own pause button and take a moment to reflect. The author hopes that by doing so readers will choose to embark on their own journey in trying to make the current (or future) workplace a better place. In closing the author asks that organizations commit themselves to bringing back the humane in a bid to preserve a well-balanced ethos that encompasses both organizational and humane aspects of working life.

REFERENCES

Adair, J (1973) *Action Centred Leadership*, McGraw-Hill, London

Adair, J (2003) *Not Bosses But Leaders: How to lead the way to success*, Kogan Page, London

Adler, NJ (1991) *International Dimensions of Organizational Behavior*, PWS-KENT Publishing Company, California

AGR (2011) Graduate Recruiter, AGR [Online] http://www.agr.org.uk/ write/Documents/GR%20Back%20Issues/2011_1.pdf

Albanese, R (1994) Team-building process: key to better project results, *Journal of Management in Engineering*, 10 (6), pp 36–44

Allen, N and Hecht, T (2001) The romance of teams: toward an understanding of its psychological underpinnings and implications, *Journal of Occupational and Organizational Psychology*, 77 (4), pp 439–61

Allport, GW (1961) *Pattern and Growth in Personality*, Rinehart & Wilson, New York

Amabile, T and Kramer, S (2010) What really motivates workers, *Harvard Business Review*, 88 (1), pp 44–45

Anderson, NR (1992) Eight decades of employment interview research: a retrospective meta-review and prospective commentary, *The European Work and Organizational Psychologist*, 2 (1), pp 1–32

Anderson, CI and Hunsaker, PL (1985) Why there's romancing at the office and why it's everybody's problem, *Personnel*, 62 (2), pp 57–63

Argyris, C (1983) Action science and intervention, *The Journal of Applied Behavioural Science*, 19 (2), pp 115–40

Armstrong, M (2009) *Handbook of Performance Management: An evidence-based guide to delivering performance*, Kogan Page, London

Arnold, J (2005) *Work Psychology: Understand human behaviour in the workplace*, Pearson Education, London

Asch, S (1951) Effects of group pressure upon the modification and distortion of judgements, in *Groups, Leadership and Men; Research in human relations*, ed H Guetzkow, pp 179–90, Carnegie Press, Oxford

Asch, S (1952) *Social Psychology*, Prentice-Hall, Englewood Cliffs

Ashman, I (2013) The face-to-face delivery of downsizing decisions in UK public sector organizations, *Public Management Review*, 14 May, pp 1–21

Avolio, B, Gardner, WL, Walumbwa, FO, Luthans, F and May, DR (2004) Unlocking the mask: a look at the process by which authentic leaders impact follower attitudes and behaviors, *The Leadership Quarterly*, 15 (6), pp 801–23

Bandler, R, Fitzpatrick, O and Roberti, A (2014) *How to Take Charge of Your Life: The user's guide to NLP*, Harper Collins, London

Banks, M and Miller, R (1984) Reliability and convergent validity of the Job Components Inventory, *Journal of Occupational Psychology*, 57 (3), pp 181–84

Barclay, J (1999) Employee selection: A question of structure, *Personnel Review*, 28, pp 134–51

Barrick, MR and Mount, MK (1991) The big five personality dimensions and job performance: a Meta-Analysis, *Personnel Psychology*, 44 (1), pp 1–26

Bassin, M (1988) Teamwork at General Foods: new and improved, *Personnel Journal*, 65 (5), pp 62–70

Belbin, M (2010) *Team Roles at Work*, Elsevier, Oxford

Belt, V, Drake, P and Chapman, K (2010) *Employability Skills: A research and policy briefing*, Commission for Employment and Skills, South Yorkshire

Bennis, W (1998) *Managing People is like Herding Cats*, Kogan Page, London

Bennis, W and Nanus, B (1985) *Leaders: The strategies for taking charge*, Harper & Row, New York

Berger, EM (1952) The relation between expressed acceptance of self and expressed acceptance of others, *Journal of Abnormal and Social Psychology*, 47 (4), pp 778–82

Berners-Lee, T and Fischetti, M (1999) *Weaving the Web: The original design and ultimate destiny of the world wide web by its inventor*, HarpersCollins, New York

Binet, A and Simon, T (1908/1916) The development of intelligence in the child, in *Development of Intelligence in Children: The Binet-Simon Scale*, ed HH Goddard, pp 182–273, Williams & Wilkins, Baltimore

Bird, J (1940) *Social Psychology*, Appleton-Century, New York

Birdwhistell, R (1971) *Kinesics and Context: Essays on body motion communication*, University of Pennsylvania Press, Philadelphia

Blake, R and Mouton, J (1964) *The Managerial Grid: Key orientations for achieving production through people*, Gulf, Houston

Blake, R and Mouton, J (1968) *Corporate Excellence through Grid Organizational Development: A systems approach*, Gulf, Houston

Blau, PM (1964) *Exchange and Power in Social Life*, Wiley, New York

Bodenhausen, GV, Sheppard, LA and Kramer, GP (1994) Negative affect and social judgment: The differential impact of anger and sadness, *European Journal of Social Psychology*, 24 (1), pp 45–62

Bowen, DE, Ledford, GE and Nathan, BR (1991) Hiring for the organization, not the job, *Academy of Management Executive*, 5 (4), pp 35–51

Boyatzis, R (1982) *The Competent Manager: A model for effective performance*, John Wiley, New York

Boyd, E and Fales, A (1983) Reflective learning, key to learning from experience, *Journal of Human Psychology*, 23 (2), pp 94–117

Brannigan, C and Humphries, D (1972) Human nonverbal behavior, a means of communication, in *Ethological studies of child behavior*, ed N Blurton Jones, pp 37–64, Cambridge University Press, New York

Bratton, J, Sawchuk, P, Forshaw, C, Callinan, M and Corbett, M (2010) *Work and Organizational Behaviour*, Palgrave MacMillan, New York

Braun, V and Clarke, V (2006) Using thematic analysis in psychology, *Qualitative Research in Psychology*, 3, pp 77–101

Brough, P and Pears, J (2004) Evaluating the influence of the type of social support on job satisfaction and work related psychological well-being, *International Journal of Organisational Behaviour*, 8 (2), pp 472–85

Burns, J (1978) *Leadership*, Harper & Row, New York

Burr, V (1995) *An Introduction to Social Constructionism*, Routledge, London

Butler, JJK, Cantrell, RS and Flick, RJ (1999) Transformational leadership behaviors, upward trust, and satisfaction in self-managed work teams, *Organization Development Journal*, 17 (1), pp 13–28

Campion, A, Medsker, GJ and Higgs, C (1993) Relation between work group characteristics and effectiveness: implications for designing an effective work group, *Personnel Psychology*, 46 (4), pp 823–50

Campion, MA, Palmer, DK and Campion, JE (1997) A review of structure in the selection interview, *Personnel Psychology*, 50 (3), pp 655–702

Carlyle, T (1840) *On Heroes, Hero-worship and the Heroic in History*, Chapman and Hall Limited, London

Carter, S and Mankoff, J (2005) When participants do the capturing: the role of media in diary studies, in *Proceedings of CHI 2005*, pp 899–908

Cartwright, D and Zander, A (1968) *Group Dynamics: Research and theory*, HarperCollins, New York

Catano, VM, Wiesner, WH, Hackett, RD and Methot, L (2012) *Recruitment and Selection in Canada*, Nelson College Indigenous

Cattell, RB (1946) *The Description and Measurement of Personality*, Harcourt, Brace and World, New York

Cattell, JM (1890) V – Mental tests and measurements, *Mind*, 59, pp 373–81

CBI (2007) [Accessed 14 July 2013] Time well spent: embedding employability in work experience, *CBI* [Online] http://www.employers-guide.org/media/20848/time_well_spent_cbi.pdf

CBI and UUK (2009) [Accessed 13 February 2012] Future fit: preparing graduates for the world of work, *CBI* [Online] http://www.bisa.ac.uk/files/Permanent%20Files/cbi_uuk_future_fit.pdf

Child, IL (1968) Personality in culture. In Borgatta, E and Lambert, WW (eds) *Handbook of Personality Theory and Research*, Rand McNally, Chicago

CIPD (2012) [Accessed 1 March 2014] Employee outlook, Winter 2011/12, *CIPD* [Online] http://www.cipd.co.uk/binaries/5756%20Employee%20Outlook%20SR%20(WEB).pdf

CIPD (2013) [Accessed 2 March 2014] Employee Outlook: autumn 2013, *CPID* [Online] http://www.cipd.co.uk/binaries/6349%20EmpOutlook%20Autumn%20(WEB).pdf

Clutterbuck, D (2007) *Coaching the Team at Work*, Nicholas Brealey Publishing, London

Collins, J (2001) Level 5 leadership: the triumph of humility and fierce resolve, *Harvard Business Review*, 79 (1), pp 66–76

Compact Oxford English Dictionary (1991) 2nd edn, Oxford University Press, Oxford

Cook, M (2009) *Personnel Selection*, John Wiley, Chichester

Costa, PT and McCrae, RR (1992) *NEO PI-R Professional Manual*, Psychological Assessment Resources, Odessa, FL

Cotton, JL (1993) *Employee Involvement: Methods for improving performance and work attitudes*, Sage, Newbury Park

Coyle-Shapiro, J and Kessler, I (2000) Consequences of the psychological contract for the employment relationship: a large scale survey, *Journal of Organizational Behaviour*, 37 (7), pp 903–30

Craig, D (2010) The workplace's impact on time use and time loss, paper presented at the Annual Meeting of the Academy of Management, Montreal, Canada

Cruz-Cunha, M, Varajao, J, Powell, P and Martinho, R (2011) *Enterprise Information Systems*, Springer, Heidelberg

Dansereau, F, Graen, G and Haga, W (1975) Vertical dyad linkage approach to leadership within formal organizations: a longitudinal investigation of the role making process, *Organizational Behaviour and Human Performance*, 13 (1), pp 46–78

Darwin, CR (1872) *The Expression of the Emotions in and Man and Animals*, John Murray, London

Dauber, D, Fink, G and Yolles, M (2012) A configuration model of organizational culture, *Sage Open 2012*, 2, pp 1–16

Davitz, JR (1964) Auditory correlates of vocal expression of emotional feeing, in *The Communication of Emotional Meaning*, ed JR Davitz, pp 101–12, McGraw Hill, New York

Deb, T (2009) *Managing HR & Ir*, Excel Books India, Dehli

De Croon, E, Sluiter, JK, Kuijer, PP and Frings-Dresen, MH (2005) The effect of office concepts on worker health and performance: a systematic review of the literature, *Ergonomics*, 48 (2), pp 119–34

De Jonge, J and Kompier, MAJ (1997) A critical examination of the demand control support model from a work psychological perspective, *International Journal of Stress Management*, 4 (4), pp 235–58

DFEE (Department for Education and Employment) (1997) *Blunkett's Call to the Nation to Join his Crusade for Jobs*, Department for Education and Employment, London

Department of Treasury IRS (2009) [Accessed 2 January 2014] 1040 Instructions, *Department of Treasury* [Online] http://www.irs.gov/pub/irs-prior/i1040-2009.pdf

Devine, I and Markiewicz, D (1990) Cross-sex relationships at work and the impact of gender stereotypes, *Journal of Business Ethics*, 9 (4–5), pp 333–38

Dirks, KT and Ferrin, DL (2002) Trust in leadership: meta-analytic findings and implications for research and practice, *Journal of Applied Psychology*, 87 (4), pp 611–28

Doyle, CE (2003) *Work and Organizational Psychology: An introduction with attitude*, Psychology Press, East Sussex

Drennan, D (1992) *Transforming Company Culture: Getting your company from where you are now, to where you want to be*, McGraw-Hill, New York

Drucker, PF (1955) *The Practice of Management*, Heinemann, London

Drucker, PF (1967) *The Effective Executive*, Harper and Row, New York

Drucker, PF (1992) *Managing the Non-profit Organization: Practices and principles*, Butterworth Heinemann, Oxford

Drucker, PF (2008) *The Essential Drucker Quotes: The best of sixty years of Peter Drucker's essential writings on management*, Harper Business, New York

Dweck, CS and Leggett, EL (1988) A socio-cognitive approach to motivation and personality, *Psychological Review*, 95 (2), pp 256–73

Dyer, W (1987) *Team Building*, Addison-Wesley Publishing Company, Reading

Dyer, W, Dyer, G and Dyer, J (2007) *Teambuilding: Proven strategies for improving team performance*, John Wiley & Sons, Hoboken

Eckhart, T (2001) *The Power of Now: A guide to spiritual enlightenment*, Hodder & Stoughton, London

Edenborough, R (2005) *Assessment Methods in Recruitment, Selection and Performance*, Kogan Page, London

Edwards, JR (1991) Person-job fit: a conceptual integration, literature review and methodological critique, in *International Review of Industrial/Organizational Psychology volume 6*, eds CL Cooper and IT Robertson, pp 283–357, Wiley, London

Elder, RW and Harris, MM (1999) *The Employment Interview Handbook*, Sage, Thousand Oaks

Elman, J (2002) *A Cultural History of Civil Service Examinations in Later Imperial China*, University of California Press, Berkeley

Ely, M, Anzul, M, Friedman, T, Garner, D and McCormack Steinmetz, A (1991) *Doing Qualitative Research: Circles within circles*, Routledge Falmer, London

Escriba-Aguir, V and Tenias-Burillo, J (2004) Psychological well-being among hospital personnel: the role of family demands and psychosocial work environment, *International Archives of Occupational and Environmental Health*, 77 (6), pp 401–08

Eurostat [Accessed 20 December 2013] Tertiary education statistics, *Eurostat* [Online] http://epp.eurostat.ec.europa.eu/statistics_explained/index.php/Tertiary_education_statistics

EWCS (2007) [Accessed 15 December 2013] Teamwork and high performance work organisation, *EWCS* [Online] http://www.eurofound.europa.eu/ewco/reports/TN0507TR01/TN0507TR01.pdf

Ewin, R (1991) The moral status of the corporation, *Journal of Business Ethics*, 10 (10), pp 749–56

Eysenck, M (1995) *Individual Differences: Normal and abnormal*, Lawrence Erlbaum Associates Publishers, Hove

Festinger, L (1954) A theory of social comparison processes, *Human Relations*, 7 (2), pp 117–40

Festinger, L, Schachter, S and Back, KW (eds) (1950) *Social Pressure in Informal Groups: A study of human factors in housing*, Harper, New York

Fiedler, F (1967) *A Theory of Leadership Effectiveness*, McGraw-Hill, New York

Fine, SA (1955) A structure of worker functions, *The Personnel and Guidance Journal*, 34 (2), pp 66–73

Fisher, R and Ury, W (1991) *Getting to Yes: Negotiating agreement without giving in*, Penguin Books, New York

Flanagan, J (1954) The critical incident technique, *Psychological Bulletin*, 51 (4), pp 1–33

Fleishman, EA (1953) The description of supervisory behavior, *Personnel Psychology*, 37 (1), pp 1–6

Fleishman, EA (1973) Twenty years of consideration and structure, in *Current developments in the study of leadership*, eds EA Fleishman and JG Hunt, Southern Illinois University Press, Carbondale

Fleishman, EA and Harris, EF (1962) Patterns of leadership behavior related to employee grievances and turnover, *Personnel psychology*, 15 (1), pp 43–56

Fleishmann, E, Harris, E and Burtt, H (1955) *Leadership and Supervision in Industry: An evaluation of a supervisory training program*, Ohio State Bureau of Educational Research, Columbus

Ford, H (1991) *Ford on Management: Harnessing the American spirit*, Wiley-Blackwell, London

Friedkin, N (1999) Choice shift and group polarization, *American Sociological Review*, **64** (6), pp 856–75

Furnham, A (2005) *The Psychology of Behaviour at Work: The individual in the organization*, Psychology Press, Hove

Gabriel, Y (2012) Organizations in a state of darkness: towards a theory of organizational miasma, *Journal of Organization Studies*, **33** (9), pp 1137–52

Gardner, J (1990) *On Leadership*, The Free Press, New York

Gautier, C (2007) Managing romance in the workplace, *Journal of Employee Assistance*, **37** (1), pp 7–9

George, B (2003) *Authentic Leadership*, Jossey Bass, San Francisco

Gersick, C (1988) Time and transition in work teams: toward a new model of group development, *Academy of Management Journal*, **31** (1), pp 9–41

Gilbreath, B and Benson, P (2004) The contribution of supervisor behaviour to employee psychological well-being, *Work & Stress*, **18** (3), pp 255–66

Goffee, R and Jones, G (1998) *The Character of a Corporation, How your company's culture can make or break your business*, HarperCollins, New York

Goleman, D (1996) *Emotional Intelligence: Why it can matter more than IQ*, Bloomsbury, London

Goodnight, R (2004) Laissez-faire leadership, in *Encyclopedia of leadership*, eds G Goethals, G Sorenson and J Burns, pp 821–24, Sage Publications, Newbury Park

Graen, G and Uhl-Bien, M (1995) Relationship based approach to leadership development of leader member exchange (LMX) theory of leadership over 25 years: applying a multi-level multi domain perspective, *Leadership Quarterly*, **6** (2), pp 219–47

Grant, E (1969) Human facial expressions, *Man*, **4** (4), pp 525–36

Greenberg, J and Baron, R (2000) *Behaviour in Organizations*, Prentice-Hall, New York

Grint, K (1998) *The Sociology of Work*, 2nd edn, Polity Press, Cambridge

Gruter, M and Masters, RD (1986) Ostracism: a social and biological phenomenon, *Ethology and Sociobiology*, **7** (3–4), pp 149–395

Hare, P (1976) *Handbook of Small Group Research*, The Free Press, New York

Harter, S (2002) Authenticity, in *Handbook of Positive Psychology*, eds CR Snyder and S Lopez, pp 382–94, Oxford University Press, Oxford

Hassan, S and Hatmaker, DM (2014) Leadership and performance of public employees: effects of the quality and characteristics of manager–employee relationships, *Journal of Public Administration Research and Theory*, **4**, pp 1–29

Hausmann, MF (1931) Otto Lipmann and industrial psychology in
    Germany, *Personnel Journal*, 9, pp 417–20

HECSU (Higher Education Career Services Unit) (2012) [Accessed 6 June
    2013] What do graduates do? 2012, *HECSU* [Online] http://
    www.hecsu.ac.uk/assets/assets/documents/WDGD_Oct_2012.pdf

Hersey, P and Blanchard, K (1969) Life cycle theory of leadership, *Journal
    of Training and Development*, 23 (5), pp 26–34

Hersey, P and Blanchard, K (1988) *Management of Organizational
    Behavior*, 5th edn, Prentice Hall, Englewood Cliffs

High Fliers (2013) [Accessed 3 January 2014] The graduate report 2013,
    High Fliers [Online] http://www.highfliers.co.uk/download/
    GMReport13.pdf

Hillage, J and Pollard, E (1998) *Developing a Framework for Policy
    Analysis*, DfEE, London

HM Treasury (1997) *Gordon Brown unveils UK employment action plan*,
    Treasury Press Release 122/97, HM Treasury, London

Hofstede, G (1980) *Culture's Consequences: International differences in
    work-related values*, Sage, Beverly Hills

Hofstede, G (1983) The cultural relativity of organizational practices and
    theories, *Journal of International Business Studies*, 14 (2), pp 75–89

Hofstede, G, Hofstede, GJ and Minkov, M (2010) *Cultures and
    Organisations: Software of the mind*, 3rd edn, McGraw-Hill,
    New York

Hofstede, G, Neuijen, B, Ohayev, DD and Sanders, G (1990) Measuring
    organizational cultures: a qualitative and quantitative study across
    twenty cases, *Administrative Science Quarterly*, 35 (2), pp 286–316

Hogg, M and Vaughan, G (2010) *Essentials of Social Psychology*, Pearson
    Education Limited, Harlow

Houdmont, J, Kerr, R and Randall, R (2012) Organisational psychosocial
    hazard exposures in UK policing: management standards indicator tool
    reference values, *Policing: an International Journal of Police Strategies
    & Management*, 35 (1), pp 182–97

Ilies, R, Morgeson, FP and Nahrgang, JD (2005) Authentic leadership and
    eudaemonic well-being: understanding leader–follower outcomes,
    The Leadership Quarterly, 16 (3), pp 373–94

Institute of Directors (2007) [Accessed 14 April 2013] Institute of directors
    skill briefing, December 2007: Graduate employability skills, *IOD*
    [Online] http://www.iod.com/MainWebSite/Resources/Document/
    policy_paper_graduates_employability_skills.pdf

ITU (2013) [Accessed 14 February 2013] World telecommunications
    ICT indication database (2006–2013), *ITU* [Online] Available from:
    http://www.itu.int/en/ITU-D/Statistics/Pages/stat/default.aspx

Jackson, J and Harkins, G (1985) Equity in effort: an explanation of the social loafing effect, *Journal of Personality and Social Psychology*, 49 (5), pp 1199–1206

James, J (1951) A preliminary study of the size determinant in small group interaction, *American Sociological Review*, 16 (4), pp 474–77

Janis, I (1972) *Victims of Group Think*, Houghton Mifflin, New York

Janis, I (1982) *Group Think: Psychological studies of policy decisions and fiascoes*, Hougton Mifflin, Boston

Jankowicz, D (2004) *An Easy Guide to Repertory Grids*, John Wiley, Hoboken

Jenkins, WO (1947) A review of leadership studies with particular reference to military problems, *Psychological Bulletin*, 44 (1), 54–79

Johnson, SC, Baxter, LC, Wilder, LS, Pipe, JG, Heiserman, JE and Prigatano, GP (2002) Neural correlates of self-reflection, *Brain*, 125 (8), pp 1808–14

Johnson, JV, Hall, EM and Theorell, T (1989) Combined effects of job strain and social isolation on cardiovascular disease morbidity and mortality in a random sample of the Swedish male working population, *Scandinavian Journal of Work, Environment & Health*, 15 (4), pp 271–79

Jones, AP, Main, DS, Butler, MC and Johnson, LA (1982) Narrative job descriptions as potential sources of job analysis ratings, *Personnel Psychology*, 35 (4), pp 813–28

Jones, SR (1990) Worker interdependence and output: The Hawthorne studies reevaluated, *American Sociological Review*, 55 (2), pp 176–90

Kahn, BE and Isen, AM (1993) The influence of positive affect on variety-seeking among safe, enjoyable products, *Journal of Consumer Research*, 20 (2), pp 257–70

Karasek, R (1979) Job demands, job decision latitude, and mental strain: implications for job redesign, *Administrative Science Quarterly*, 24 (2), pp 285–308

Karasek, R and Theorell, T (1990) *Healthy Work: Stress, productivity, and the reconstruction of working life*, Basic Books, New York

Karau, S and Williams, K (1993) A meta analytic review and theoretical integration, *Journal of Personality and Social Psychology*, 65 (4), pp 681–706

Kark, R and Shamir, B (2002) The dual effect of transformational leadership: priming relational and collective selves and further effects on followers, in *Transformational and Charismatic Leadership: The road ahead*, eds BJ Avolio and FJ Yammarino, pp 7–91, Elsevier, Oxford

Katz, D, Maccoby, N and Morse, NC (1950) *Productivity, Supervision and Morale in an Office Situation Part 1*, Institute for Social Research, Oxford

Kelly, GA (1955/1963) *The Psychology of Personal Constructs*, Norton, New York

Kelman, HC (1958) Compliance, identification, and internalization: three processes of attitude change, *The Journal of Conflict Resolution*, 2 (1), pp 51–60

Kessler, R (2006) *Competency Based Interview*, Career Press Inc, Franklin Lakes

Kim, H and Markus, HR (1999) Deviance or uniqueness, harmony or conformity? A cultural analysis, *Journal of Personality and Social Psychology*, 77 (4), pp 785–800

Kirkpatrick, S and Locke, A (1991) Leadership: do traits matter? *Academy of Management Executive*, 5 (2), pp 48–60

Kristof, AL (1996) Person-organization fit: an integrative review of its conceptualizations, measurement and implications, *Personnel Psychology*, 49 (1), pp 1–49

La Barre, W (1947) The cultural basis of emotions and gestures, *Journal of Personality*, 16 (1), pp 49–68

Lacoursiere, R (1980) *The Life Cycle of Groups: Group development stage theory*, Human Sciences Press, New York

Latane, B, Williams, K and Harkins, S (1979) Many hands make light the work: the causes and consequences of social loafing, *Journal of personality and social psychology*, 37 (6), pp 822–32

Lawson, B and Samson, D (2001) Developing innovation capability in organisations: a dynamic capabilities approach, *International Journal of Innovation Management*, 5 (3), pp 377–400

Leaman, A and Bordass, W (2005) Productivity in buildings: the 'killer' variables, 2nd revision, *Ecolibrium*, pp 16–20

Leckie, NA, Léonard, A, Tureotte, J and Wallace, D (2001) *Employer and Employee Perspectives on Human Resource Practices*, Statistics Canada Report 71-584-MPF No 1, Canada, Statistics Canada

Lee, SY and Brand, JL (2005) Effects of control over office workspace on perceptions of the work environment and work outcomes, *Journal of Environmental Psychology*, 25 (3), pp 323–33

Lerner, G (1986) *The Creation of Patriarchy*, Oxford University Press, Oxford

Leslie, A (1987) Pretense and representation: the origins of 'Theory of Mind', *Psychological Review*, 94 (4), pp 412–26

Lewicki, R, Barry, B and Saunders, DN (2001) *Essentials of Negotiation*, McGraw Hill, New York

Lewin, K, Lippitt, R and White, R (1939) Patterns of aggressive behaviour in experimentally created social climates, *Journal of Social Psychology*, 10 (2), pp 271–301

Lippitt, R and White, R (1943) The 'social climate' of children's groups, in *Child Behaviour and Development*, eds R Barker, J Kounin and H Wright, pp 485–508, McGraw-Hill, New York

Locke, E and Latham, GP (2004) What should we do about motivation theory? Six recommendations for the twenty-first century, *Academy of Management Review*, **29** (3), pp 388–403

Lord, RG, De Vader, CL and Alliger, GM (1986) A meta-analysis of the relation between personality traits and leadership perceptions: an application of validity generalization procedures, *Journal of Applied Psychology*, **71** (3), pp 402–10

Luthans, F (1995) *Organisational behaviour*, 7th edn, McGraw Hill, New York

Maguire, H (2002) Psychological contracts: are they still relevant? *Career Development International*, 7 (3), pp 167–80

Mann, L (1969) *Social Psychology*, Wiley, New York

Marquardt, MJ (2002) *Building the Learning Organization: Mastering the five elements for corporate learning*, Davies-Black Press, Palo Alto

Maslow, A (1954) *Motivation and Personality*, Harper and Row, New York

Maurer, S, Sue-Chan, C and Latham, GP (1999) The situational interview, in *The Employment Interview Handbook*, eds RW Eder and MM Harris, pp 159–77, Sage, Thousand Oaks

Mausner-Dorsch, H and Eaton, WW (2000) Psychosocial work environment and depression: epidemiologic assessment of the demand-control model, *American Journal of Public Health*, **90** (11), pp 1765–70

Mayo, E (1945) *The Social Problems of an Industrial Civilization*, Ayer, New Hampshire

McCormick, EJ and Jeanneret, PR (1988) Position Analysis Questionnaire (PAQ), in *The Job Analysis Handbook for Business and Industry*, ed S Gael, pp 825–42, Wiley, New York

McClelland, D (1973) Testing for competence rather than for intelligence, *American Psychologist*, **28** (1), pp 1–14

McGregor, D (1960) *The Human Side of Enterprise*, McGraw-Hill, New York

Mehrabian, A (1972) *Nonverbal Communications*, Aldine Atherton, New York

Mehrabian, A (2007) *Nonverbal Communications*, Transaction Publishers, New Jersey

Mezirow, J (1992) *Transformative Dimensions of Adult Learning*, Jossey-Bass, San Francisco

Millar, R, Crute, V and Hargee, O (1992) *Professional Interviewing*, Routledge, London

Miller, D (1987) Strategic industrial relations and human resource management: distinction, definition and recognition, *Journal of Management Studies*, **24** (4), pp 347–61

Mintzberg, H, Raisinghani, D and Theoret, A (1976) The structure of 'unstructured' decision processes, *Administrative Science Quarterly*, 21 (2), pp 246–75

Moon, J (2003) *Reflection in Learning and Professional Development*, Kogan Page, London

Morgan, G (1998) *Images of Organizations: The executive edition*, Berrett-Koehler, San Francisco

Mueller, F, Procter, S and Buchanan, D (2000) Teamworking in its context(s): antecedents, nature and dimensions, *Human Relations*, 53 (11), pp 1387–1424

Munsterberg, H (1913) *Psychology and Industrial Efficiency*, Houghton Mifflin Company, London

Myers, C (1929) *Industrial Psychology*, Thornton Butterworth, London

Myers, IB and Myers, PB (1980) *Gifts Visible*, Consulting Psychologists Press, Palo Alto

NCIHE (1997) *The Dearing Report*, The National Committee of Enquiry into Higher Education, London

Newcomb, TM (1956) The prediction of interpersonal attraction, *American Psychologist*, 11 (11), 575–86

Ng, KY and Van Dyne, L (2001) Individualism-collectivism as a boundary condition for effectiveness of minority influence in decision making, *Organizational Behavior and Human Decision Processes*, 84 (2), 198–225

OBR (2012) [Accessed 30 October 2013] Economic and fiscal outlook March 2012, *OBR* [Online] http://cdn.budgetresponsibility.independent. gov.uk/March-2012-EFO.pdfECD

ONS (2012a) [Accessed 30 March 2013] Graduates in the labour market 2012, *OECD* [Online] http://www.ons.gov.uk/ons/dcp171776_259049.pdf

ONS (2012b) [Accessed 20 February 2013] Public sector employment, Q4 2012, *ONS* [Online] http://www.ons.gov.uk/ons/rel/pse/public-sector-employment/q4-2012/stb-pse-2012q4.html

ONS (2012c) [Accessed 25 February 2013] UK Business: activity, Size, Location 2012, *ONS* [Online] http://www.ons.gov.uk/ons/rel/bus-register/uk-business/2012/index.html

ONS (2013) [Accessed 14 February 2013] Internet access-households and individuals, *ONS* [Online] http://www.ons.gov.uk/ons/dcp171778_322713.pdf

Otten, S, Sassenberg, K and Kessler, T (2009) *Intergroup Relations: The role of motivation and emotion*, Psychology Press, Hove

Panel of Fair Access to the Professions (2009) [Accessed 13 February 2012] Unleashing aspiration: the final report of the panel on fair access to the professions, *Panel of Fair Access to the Professions* [Online] http://www.bis.gov.uk/policies/higher-education/access-to-professions/panel-on-fair-access-professions

Parducci, A and Fabre, J (1995) Contextual effects in judgement and choice, in *Contributors to Decision Making*, eds JP Caverni, F Barron and H Jungermann, pp 97–109, Elsevier Publishers, Amsterdam

Parker, G (2003) *Cross-functional Teams: Working with allies, enemies and other strangers*, Jossey-Bass, San Francisco

Pierce, CA (1998) Factors associated with participating in a romantic relationship in a work environment, *Journal of Applied Social Psychology*, 28 (18), pp 1712–30

Pierce, CA and Aguinis, H (2003) Romantic relationships in organizations: a test of a model of formation and impact factors, *Management Research: The Journal of the Iberoamerican Academy of Management*, 1 (2), pp 161–69

Pierce, CA, Byrne, D and Aguinis, H (1996) Attraction in organizations: a model of workplace romance, *Journal of Organizational Behavior*, 17 (1), pp 5–32

Ployhart, RE (2012) The psychology of competitive advantage: an adjacent possibility, *Industrial and Organizational Psychology: Perspectives on Science and Practice*, 5, pp 62–81

Ployhart, RE and Holtz, BC (2008) The diversity–validity dilemma: strategies for reducing racioethnic and sex subgroup differences and adverse impact in selection, *Personnel Psychology*, 61 (1), pp 153–72

Poole, M (1983) Decision development in small groups: a comparison of two models, *Communication Monographs*, 48 (1), pp 1–24

Powell, GN and Foley, S (1998) Something to talk about: romantic relationships in organizational settings, *Journal of Management*, 24 (3), pp 421–48

Preston, A (1991) Occupational gender segregation: trends and explanations, *The Quarterly Review of Economics and Finance*, 39, pp 611–24

Quinn, RE (1977) Coping with Cupid: the formation, impact, and management of romantic relationships in organizations, *Administrative Science Quarterly*, 22 (1), pp 30–45

Rainsbury, E, Hodges, D, Burchell, N and Lay, MC (2002) Ranking workplace competencies: student and graduate perceptions, *Asia-Pacific Journal of Cooperative Education*, 3 (2), pp 8–18

Reich, RB (2002) *The Future of Success*, Vintage, London

Ringelmann, M (1913) Reserches sur les moteurs animes: travail de l'homme, *Annales de l'Institut National Agronomique*, 2 (12), pp 1–40

Robbins, S (2001) *Organisational Behaviour*, Prentice-Hall, New Jersey

Robertson, IT and Smith, M (2001) Personnel selection, *Journal of Occupational and Organizational Psychology*, 74 (4), pp 441–72

Rodger, A (1952) The seven-point plan, Issue 1, National Institute of Industrical Psychology

Roethlisberger, FJ and Dickson, WJ (1939) *Management and the Worker: An account of a research*, Harvard University Press, Cambridge

Rogers, C (1951) *Client-centered Therapy: Its current practice, implications and theory*, Constable, London

Rogers, C (1961) *On Becoming a Person: A therapist's view of psychotherapy*, Constable, London

Rosenbaum, M (1986) Comment on a proposed two-stage theory of relationship formation: first, repulsion; then, attraction, *Journal of Personality and Social Psychology*, 51 (6), pp 1171–72

Rosenberg, MJ, Hovland, CI, McGuire, WJ, Abelson, RP and Brehn, JW (1960) *Attitude Organization Change*, Yale University Press, New Haven

Rosenthal, R and DePaulo, BM (1979) Sex differences in eavesdropping on nonverbal cues, *Journal of Personality and Social Psychology*, 37 (2), pp 273–85

Rosse, JG, Stecher, MD, Miller, JL and Levin, RA (1998) The impact of response distortion on preemployment personality testing and hiring decisions, *Journal of Applied Psychology*, 83 (4), pp 634–44

Rousseau, D (1995) *Psychological Contracts in Organizations: Understanding written and unwritten agreements*, Sage, California

Rowe, C (1995) Clarifying the use of competence and competency models in recruitment, assessment and staff development, *Industrial and Commercial Training*, 27 (11), pp 12–17

Ruesch, J (1966) Social process, *Archives of General Psychiatry*, 15 (6), pp 577–89

Ryan, DS (1983) Self-esteem: an operational definition and ethical analysis, *Journal of Psychology and Theology*, 11 (4), pp 295–302

Sagiv, L and Schwartz, SH (2007) Cultural values in organisations: insights for Europe, *European Journal of International Management*, 1 (3), pp 176–90

Samons, D and Lawson, B (2001) Developing innovational capability in organisations: a dynamic capabilities approach, *International Journal of Innovation Management*, 5 (3), pp 377–400

Sandberg, J (2000) Understanding human competence at work: an interpretative approach, *Academy of management Journal*, 43 (1), pp 9–25

Sandberg, S (2013) *Lean in: Women, work and the will to lead*, WH Allen, United Kingdom

Sathe, V (1983) Implications of corporate culture: a manager's guide to action, *Organizational Dynamics*, 11 (2), pp 4–23

Saville & Holdsworth Ltd (1995) *Working Profiling System*, Saville & Holdsworth, London

Schein, EH (1990) Organizational culture, *American Psychologist*, 45 (2), pp 109–19

Schein, EH (2010) *Organizational Culture and Leadership*, Jossey-Bass, San Francisco

Schmidt, F and Hunter, J (1998) The validity and utility of selection methods in personnel psychology: Practical and theoretical implications of 85 years of research findings, *Psychological Bulletin*, **124** (2), pp 262–74

Schutte, NS, Malouff, JM, Bobik, C, Coston, TD, Greeson, C, Jedlicka, C, Rhodes, E and Wendorf, G (2001) Emotional intelligence and interpersonal relations, *The Journal of Social Psychology*, **141** (4), pp 523–36

Seers, A and Woodruff, S (1997) Temporal pacing in task forces: group development or deadline pressure? *Journal of Management*, **23** (2), pp 169–87

Senge, P (1990) The leader's new work: building learning organizations, *Sloan Management Review*, **32** (1), pp 7–23

Shackleton, V and Newell, S (1997) International assessment and selection, in *International Handbook of Selection and Assessment*, eds N Anderson and P Herriot, Wiley, Chichester

Shahani, C, Dipboye, R and Gehrlein, T (1993) Attractiveness bias in the interview: exploring the boundaries of an effect, *Basic and Applied Social Psychology*, **14** (3), pp 317–28

Shapira, Z (1995) *Risk Taking: A managerial perspective*, Russell Sage Foundation, New York

Shaver, KG (1977) *Principles of Social Psychology*, Winthrop, Cambridge

Shaw, ME (1955) A comparison of two types of leadership in various communication nets, *The Journal of Abnormal and Social Psychology*, **50** (1), pp 127–34

Sherif, M (1936) *The Psychology of Social Norms*, Harper, Oxford

Silvester, J and Chapman, AJ (1996) Unfair discrimination in the selection interview: an attributional account, *International Journal of Selection and Assessment*, **4** (2), pp 63–70

Smith, A (1776) *An Inquiry into the Nature and Causes of the Wealth of Nations*

Smith, M and Smith, P (2005) *People at Work: Competencies in psychometric testing*, BPS and Blackwell Publishing, Oxford

Smith, PB *et al* (1994) Organizational event management in 14 countries: a comparison with Hofstede's dimensions, in *Journeys in Cross-cultural Psychology*, eds F Van der Vijver, P Schmitz and P Boski, pp 372–81, Swets & Zeitlinger, Amsterdam

Sparrowe, RT (2005) Authentic leadership and the narrative self, *The Leadership Quarterly*, **16** (3), pp 419–39

Spiegel, J and Torres, C (1994) *Manager's Official Guide to Team Working*, Pfeiffer, San Diego

Stansfeld, SA, Fuhrer, R, Shipley, MJ and Marmot, MG (1999) Work characteristics predict psychiatric disorder: prospective results from the Whitehall II study, *Occupational and Environmental Medicine*, **56** (5), pp 302–07

Stark, E, Shaw, J and Duffy, M (2007) Preference for group work, winning orientation, and social loafing, *Group & Organization Management*, **32** (6), pp 699–723

Steiner, I (1972) *Group Process and Productivity*, Academic Press, New York

Stogdill, RM (1948) Personal factors associated with leadership: a survey of the literature, *Journal of Psychology*, **25** (1), pp 35–71

Stogdill, RM (1970) Personal factors associated with leadership: a survey of literature, in *Leadership*, ed CA Gibb, Penguin, Harmondsworth

Stogdill, RM (1974) *Handbook of Leadership: A survey of theory and research*, Free Press, New York

Tajfel, H (1979) Individuals and groups in social psychology, *British Journal of Social and Clinical Psychology*, **18** (2), pp 183–90

Tate, DS (1994) Restructuring agency job descriptions using realistic job previews, *Administration and Policy in Mental Health and Mental Health Services Research*, **22** (2), pp 169–73

Taylor, FW (1919) *The Principles of Scientific Management*, Harper & Brothers Publishers, New York and London

Thorndike, EL (1920) A constant error in psychological ratings, *Journal of Applied Psychology*, **4** (1), pp 25–29

Tjosvold, D (1991) *Team Organization: An enduring competitive advantage*, Wiley, London

Tolle, E (2001) *The Power of Now: A guide to spiritual enlightenment*, Hodder Paperbacks, London

Torrington, D, Hall, L, Taylor, S and Atkinson, C (2005) *Human Resource Management*, Pearson Education, London

Tuckman, B (1965) Developmental sequence in small groups, *Psychological Bulletin*, **63** (6), pp 384–99

Tuckman, B and Jensen, M (1977) Stages of small group development, *Group and Organizational Studies*, **2** (4), pp 419–27

Turner, J (1996) *Social Influence*, Open University Press, Milton Keynes

Twenge, JM (2007) *Generation Me: Why today's young Americans are more confident*, assertive, entitled – and more miserable than ever before, Free Press, New York

UKCES (2009) *Ambition 2020: World class skills and jobs for the UK*, UKCES, Wath-upon-Dearne

Van der Doef, M and Maes, S (1999) The job demand-control (-support) model and psychological well-being: a review of 20 years of empirical research, *An International Journal of Work*, Health & Organisations, **13** (2), pp 87–114

Vroom, V and Jago, A (1988) *The New Leadership: Managing participation in organizations*, Prentice-Hall, New York

Warr, PB (1990) Decision latitude, job demands, and employee well-being, *Work & Stress*, 4 (4), pp 285–94

Wesselmann, ED, Wirth, JH, Pryor, JB, Reeder, GD and Williams, KD (2012) When do we ostracize? *Social Psychology and Personality Science*, 1, pp 168–74

West, M (2004) *Effective Teamwork: Practical lessons from organizational research*, BPS and Blackwell Publishing, Oxford

Williams, KD, Cheung, CKT and Choi, W (2000) Cyber ostracism: effects of being ignored over the internet, *Journal of Personality and Social Psychology*, 79, 748–62

Wilmott, B (2011) [Accessed 8 April 2014] Employees relegate job satisfaction to second place behind pay and benefits as rising cost of living bites: quarterly CIPD employee outlook survey, *CIPD* [Online] http://www.cipd.co.uk/pressoffice/press-releases/employees-relegate-job.aspx

Zajonc, RB (1968) Attitudinal effects of mere exposure, *Journal of Personality and Social Psychology Monograph Supplement*, 9 (2), pp 1–27

Zaleznik, A (1977) *Managers and Leaders: Are they different?* Harvard Business School Publications, Boston

The author is grateful to the following for permission to reproduce copyright material:

- Professor Dean Tjosvold for the Team Organization Model;
- Jeff Dyer and Kathe Sweeney of John Wiley & Sons for the Four Cs model;
- John Walkley Associates.

Every effort has been made to trace all copyright holders, but if any have been inadvertently overlooked, the publisher would be pleased to make the necessary arrangements at the first opportunity.

INDEX

NB: page numbers in *italic* indicate figures or tables

CPSIA information can be obtained at www.ICGtesting.com
Printed in the USA
LVOW10s1606180315

431078LV00006B/99/P